PRAISE FOR *THE RADICAL MIND*

"Three decades after the collapse of the Soviet Union, we are witnessing in this country an astonishing revival of the Marxist totalitarian mindset, and it is taking over our institutions. Raised by Communists, David Horowitz understands this tyrannical worldview better than anyone, and his new book *The Radical Mind* is a harrowing journey through the corridors of the twenty-first century totalitarianism that goes by the name of progressivism. Must reading!"

> —**Dinesh D'Souza**, *New York Times* bestselling author and filmmaker

"Many sober and dedicated patriots, throw up their hands when it comes to describing Woke ideas and agendas which are systematically eating away the foundations of our democracy, calling them 'crazy' and 'deranged.' David Horowitz, who was once one of their intellectual leaders knows differently. His new book, *The Radical Mind* unveils the sinister logic of their strategy and how it has already undermined the foundations of our American system, which they hate."

> —**Mark R. Levin**, *New York Times* bestselling author of *Unfreedom of the Press*

"David Horowitz has written an insightful, compelling, and ultimately troubling book about the leftist mindset. An important read."

> —**Peter Schweizer**, #1 *New York Times* bestselling author of *Red-Handed*

"Once again, David Horowitz makes it clear why, for over half a century, he has been the preeminent explainer and documentarian of the American Left and its attempt to destroy America. Unlike any other country, America is not a race or an ethnicity. It is an idea. Therefore, it is in some ways easier to destroy America than it is to destroy most other countries. All you have to do is destroy its ideas. How and why the left is doing this is brilliantly and concisely set forth in this book. If Aladdin granted me three wishes, one of them would be that every American read this book."

> —**Dennis Prager**, nationally syndicated radio talk show host, cofounder of PragerU, and bestselling author of *The Rational Bible*

"David Horowitz has written eloquently for the last half-century about the dangers the Left poses to America, especially the legacy bequeathed by the destructive 1960s generation. Now he astutely shows that the current woke era of radical cultural Marxism is an even greater threat to America, given our revolutionaries are not just in the street, but now are the establishment and control all the major levers of institutional power and influence. A chilling, incisive, and timely warning to America to wake up before it's too late from our most knowledgeable analyst of the America Left."

> —**Victor Davis Hanson**, The Hoover Institution and *New York Times* bestselling author of *The Dying Citizen*

"A brilliant take down of the Democrat party—the party of slavery; the confederacy; Jim Crow; Dred Scott; the Southern Manifesto; that, as a percentage of the House and Senate, voted *less* for the Civil Rights Act of 1964 than did Republicans; that, due to the "war on poverty," launched in the mid 1960s, has devastated the nuclear family and created an epidemic of fatherlessness; and the party that opposes school choice."

　　—**Larry Elder**, nationally syndicated radio talk show host,
　　　and bestselling author

"David Horowitz is a modern legend. This book is critical to understanding the Left and how we defeat them."

　　—**Charlie Kirk**, founder and president of
　　　Turning Point USA, and *New York Times*
　　　bestselling author of *The MAGA Doctrine*

THE
RADICAL
MIND

THE RADICAL MIND

THE DESTRUCTIVE PLANS OF THE WOKE LEFT

DAVID HOROWITZ

Humanix Books
www.humanixbooks.com

To my wife April whose love—
constant and extravagant—
has been my support through
all the ordeals of this life . . .

And to our family—our remarkable children
and grandchildren—and our extended family,
Laura, Nikki, and Trinity—who have rewarded
our days with light and laughter, thank you.

CONTENTS

ONE   Heading Towards the Abyss   1

TWO   Ideology Über Alles   23

THREE   White Skin Privilege   45

FOUR   Existential Threat   71

FIVE   A Tsunami of Hate   95

SIX   Progressive Blindness   107

CODA   Defense of the Republic   137

Notes   141

Acknowledgments   159

Index   161

THE
RADICAL
MIND

ONE

HEADING TOWARDS THE ABYSS

Within the Revolution everything;
outside of it nothing.

FIDEL CASTRO

THE CRISIS FACING OUR nation is a crisis of faith—faith in the Constitution that has shaped our destiny, faith in individual freedom and accountability, faith in the principle of equality before the law.

The root cause of the lawlessness consuming America is the monopoly of executive power in Washington and in America's urban centers by a party that has fallen under the control of a Marxist left that believes in breaking the law for the sake of "social justice" and puts its faith in the supremacy of the state.

This left describes itself as "progressive," but it is inspired by views that are hundreds of years old and have been discredited wherever they have been put into practice. Progressives are focused on "re-imagining" American institutions and principles to conform to an ideological conception of the future that they describe as "equitable" and "socially just." To achieve this future, the left's first goal is to dismantle the constitutional order that has created the prosperity and freedoms that have grown and spread since the American founding. The left views this order as "racist," "oppressive," and in need of a "fundamental transformation."

Having been born into this political left and then rejected it, I am familiar with its seductive public message, and its sinister concealed intentions. I am also in a position to assess the threat it poses to the American future, which is grave.

I was raised by card-carrying Communists, who always and only referred to themselves as progressives and were sworn enemies of America and its institutions, as was I. We saw ourselves as revolutionary warriors, acting on the right side of history.

We could not have been more mistaken. The "moral arc" of history is not "bent towards justice," as progressives maintain, and there is no "right side" to be on. If there were, the twentieth century would have been the most enlightened one, instead of the scene of the greatest atrocities and oppressions on human record. Worse yet for this progressive myth, these atrocities and oppressions were mainly perpetrated by progressives themselves, acting in the name of social justice.

The practical achievement of the revolutionaries was the dismantling of whole societies, and their reconstruction as national prisons and slave labor camps, in which every aspect of life was controlled by the state. Supported by progressives the world over, Communists bankrupted entire continents and killed more than 100 million people—in peacetime—in order to realize their radical schemes.[1]

Their atrocities and failures continued for more than 70 years, until the day they saw their progressive future collapse under its own weight. This failure was entirely predictable because, as every similar attempt to "re-imagine society" and change it by force has shown, it is simply beyond the power of human beings who are the true source of *in*justice to create a world that is just.

Forty years ago, a series of tragic events, involving the murder of innocents by a progressive vanguard, stopped me in my tracks and caused me to re-evaluate what I had believed until then. These second thoughts turned me against the cause to which I had been devoted since my youth, and which I now saw as a threat to everything human beings hold dear.

However, most of my generation of radicals chose to continue on their destructive course. Over the next decades, I watched the radical movement I was born into infiltrate and then take control of the Democratic Party and the nation's cultural institutions, until one of its own, Barack Obama, became president of the United States and promised to fundamentally transform it.

From the moment I joined the conservative right forty years ago, I was impressed—and also alarmed—by the disparity in political rhetoric used by the two sides fighting this fateful conflict. My radical comrades and I had always viewed these battles as episodes in a war conducted by other means, even as our opponents failed to understand that they were in a war at all.

Our rhetoric proclaimed our goals to be "peace," "equality," and "justice." But this was always a deception. We used politically lethal terms that demonized our opponents as "racists," and "oppressors." We did so because we believed that our goals could only be achieved by vanquishing our opponents so completely that we could get to the work of destroying America's constitutional order and replacing it with our socialist fantasies. The word "fantasy" here is precise in this context because two hundred years of socialist movements have never produced a socialist plan that actually works.

The U.S. Constitution valorizes political compromise and is built on the defense of individual rights, most prominently the rights to own property and express oneself freely. America's founders regarded property ownership as the basis of private independence from the state, and therefore of individual freedom. By contrast, we radicals regarded property as the root cause of the evils that oppressed us. Consequently, the principles we operated under were not the same as those to which we gave lip service in order to win public support.

The Bolshevik revolutionary Leon Trotsky explained our attitude in a famous pamphlet called *Their Morals and Ours*.[2] Their morals, he denigrated as "bourgeois" morality, based on class values that served the oppressors. One can hear the same sophistry today in the left's attacks on meritocracy and performance standards as "racist," and in their demands for equal outcomes regardless of whether they are earned or not.

While Trotsky claimed that "their morals" served a ruling class, "our morals" allegedly served the people, and therefore justice. Because we believed these fictions, our morals were by default Machiavellian: *The end justified the means.*

Trotsky's pamphlet was, in fact, a desperate attempt to avoid admitting that there was anything amoral or immoral in his cynically self-serving outlook. He did so by denying the existence of moral principles, claiming instead that all morality was self-interested and designed to serve a class interest.

"Whoever does not care to return to Moses, Christ or Mohammed," i.e., to accept universal moral standards, Trotsky argued, "must acknowledge that morality is a product of social development; that there is nothing invariable about it; that it serves social interests; that these interests are contradictory; that morality more than any other form of ideology has a class character."

But this is just an admission that our morals were accurately summarized as, "the end justifies the means." The future we imagined we were creating was so desirable that achieving it justified any methods required to get there, which included the lies that hid our destructive purposes, and the atrocities they led to. Nearly a century earlier, the Russian revolutionary Georgi Plekhanov put it this way: *salus revolutiae supreme lex*—whatever the revolution demands is the supreme law.[3] In my lifetime, Cuba's sadistic dictator, Fidel Castro, notoriously proclaimed: "Within the Revolution everything; outside of it nothing."[4]

The full import of this belief was brought home to me in the spring of 1975 when our so-called anti-war movement forced America out of Indochina, allowing the North Vietnamese and Cambodian Communists to win. For more than a decade, we had claimed to care about the people of Indochina, championed their rights to self-determination, and condemned the war as a case of American imperialism and racism oppressing Asian victims.

Massive demonstrations at the Pentagon and elsewhere were designed to show our support. Pictures of Communist heroes, like Madame Nguyen Thi Binh, adorned college dormitory walls; Jane Fonda and Tom Hayden named their son after a Communist assassin, Nguyen van Troi.[5] America's radical college organization, Students for a Democratic Society, called the Communist Vietcong "the vanguard of the revolution."

By the time America withdrew from the conflict and abandoned its Indo-Chinese allies, I already knew that Communism was a monstrous evil. But I remained a supporter of the anti-war cause, and of the rights of the Indochinese to self-determination. To defend the commitments I had made, I deluded myself into believing that self-determination meant the Cambodians and Vietnamese should be able to choose even this evil if they wanted to.

This was all sophistry, because I knew that the Communists would not give them an inch of space in which to breathe free. The end that justified my position was that, like my comrades, I believed that America was the world's arch imperialist power and that its defeat was an absolute good.

What I was not prepared for were the moral depths to which the movement I had been part of had sunk. These depths were revealed in the events that followed the Communist victory. When America left Cambodia and Vietnam, the Communists proceeded to slaughter between two and three million peasants who were politically incorrect and did not welcome their Communist "solutions." It was the largest genocide since Hitler's extermination of the Jews. In Cambodia, they killed everyone who wore glasses on the grounds that as readers of books, they would transmit the oppressive ideas of the past and obstruct the progressive future.

After the Communists conquered the country, our indigenous heroine Madame Binh disappeared. No one asked after her or demanded to know her fate. As the genocidal slaughter proceeded, prominent leftists like Noam Chomsky provided cover for the Communists' crimes by denying that the atrocities were taking place.

More disturbingly, *there was not a single demonstration to protest the slaughter.* This silence unmasked the radical activists who claimed to be "anti-war" and to care about the Cambodians and Vietnamese. It showed the true agendas of the movement I had been part of.

My comrades' abandonment of the peoples and principles they claimed to defend showed definitively that the anti-war movement was never really anti-war. It was *anti-American*. It wanted America to lose and the Communists to win. And that was all it was prepared to fight for. Progressives had lied about the nature of their movement and its agendas in order to accomplish their real goal, which was the fundamental transformation of America and the creation of a socialist state.

I had known this to be the case for many years but had accepted the lies because they had served what I had imagined was a noble end. But when the lies led to embracing a genocide of the innocent, I realized that the movement I had been part of for my whole life was evil.

On my way out of the left, I spent several years re-thinking what I had believed, and trying to understand the nature of the cause that I had served. Perhaps my most profound, and certainly most disturbing, conclusion was that revolutionaries were by nature—and of necessity—criminals, who would routinely lie and break laws to achieve their ends. Every radical who believed in a revolution or a re-imagining of society from the ground up, every progressive who believed in a fundamental transformation of America, as Barack Obama described his own agenda on the eve of his 2008 election, was a criminal who did not believe in the laws that existed and was waiting to strike.

America's Constitution includes methods to amend it, and therefore to reform our social order when and where changes are needed. In making such changes, there are procedures to ensure that they represent the will of the American people and are done lawfully. But revolutionaries do not respect a constitutional order created by rich white men.

Radicals believe instead that social justice requires them to dismantle the social order, and "due process" along with it. Radicals are not reformers willing to make their changes within the framework of the law. In the name of social justice, they refuse to be bound by the regulations and procedures that an unjust and oppressive ruling class has created. *The end justifies the means.*

President Obama was raised by communists, and like me, was a committed member of the New Left. A constitutional law professor, Obama decided to break America's immigration laws and grant 800,000 illegals resident status. Before he did so, he admitted publicly on at least twenty-two recorded occasions that he had no constitutional authority to do so—*none.*[6]

So great was the pressure from radicals to break the law by preventing the illegals from being deported, that Obama felt he had to publicly explain to them that the Constitution and subsequent statutory law prohibited him from doing so. Immigration laws were a matter for Congress to change. As president, he had no authority to declare an amnesty for people illegally residing in the United States.[7] In fact, the prosperous, opportunity-rich country that illegal immigrants wished to join was created by such constitutional limits to governmental authority.

"America is a nation of laws," Obama explained on one occasion, "which means I, as the President, am obligated to enforce the law. I don't have a choice about that. . . . With respect to the notion that I can just suspend deportations through executive order, that's just not the case, because they are laws on the books that Congress has passed. . . ."[8] On another occasion, he reminded people, "I swore an oath to uphold the laws on the books. . . ."[9] And on yet another, he said: "Now, I know some people want me to bypass Congress and change the laws on my own. Believe me, the idea of doing things on my own is very tempting. I promise you. . . . But that's not how our system works. That's not how our democracy functions. That's not how our Constitution is written."[10]

When pretending to defend the American system suited his ends, Obama was a sophisticated, shrewd-enough politician to understand its rationale and functions. But he himself was a born-and-bred radical, and he didn't believe in the system itself or the constitutional restraints the Founders had created.[11] For the same reason, his civics lectures about what the Constitution authorized fell on deaf ears among radical audiences. That's what makes radicals radical: their contempt for the legal system and determination to destroy it, and to do so by circumventing, undermining, and ignoring its prescriptions. They had no desire to obey the Constitution or merely amend it.

On June 15, 2012, Obama did what he had repeatedly said the law and the Constitution barred him from doing. He issued an executive branch memorandum called the Deferred Action for Childhood Arrivals (DACA). This unilateral executive action provided a provisional amnesty for 800,000 youth who had entered the United States illegally as minors and were still under the age of 31 as of June 2012. DACA allowed these individuals to gain temporary legal status, work permits, access to publicly funded social services, and protection from deportation.[12] In fact, all of those privileges were unconstitutional and illegal.

Two years later, having witnessed scant resistance from Republicans, and gotten away with his illegal action, Obama decided to expand the scope of his crime. He undertook a second executive action, this time granting provisional amnesty to four million illegal aliens under the Deferred Action for Parents of Americans and Lawful Permanent Residents (DAPA)—an expansion of DACA.[13]

That opened the floodgates to the destructive invasion of the country we are witnessing today, although it had to wait several years until Joe Biden destroyed America's borders by illegal and unconstitutional executive actions on the first day of his presidency and invited everyone in the Western Hemisphere, including unaccompanied minors, to enter America anonymously. The invitation was ultimately extended to the entire world. And so the United States was fundamentally and illegally and unconstitutionally transformed by a party completely dominated by progressives who regarded the Constitution as a "white supremacist" contract and therefore had no respect for its Constitution or its laws.

To Obama and his party, violating the fundamental law of the land was justified because the system that had created the law was, in their eyes, oppressive and unjust—racist. (*Nota Bene:* The words "white" and "black" do not appear in the Constitution.) In committing this crime against the nation he led, Obama was guided by a radical ideology that justified the illegal means as a victory for social justice.

As a former radical, I understood how high the stakes were with Obama's election. Since the right was defending America's freedoms while the left was paying lip service to patriotic pieties but intending nothing less than the destruction of its constitutional order, I also understood that the rhetorical disparity between the two camps posed a grave threat to America's future.

In fighting this cold war, progressives regularly demonized Republicans as "racists," "white supremacists," "insurrectionists," "Nazis," and "traitors." Republicans have responded to these reckless attacks by calling Democrats "liberals" and similarly in accurate and tepid retorts. For example, they describe Democrats as "soft on crime."

Democrats are not *soft* on crime. They are *pro*-crime: Democrat district attorneys have systematically refused to prosecute violent criminals; Democrat mayors and governors have released tens of thousands of violent criminals from America's prisons and abolished cash bail so that criminals are back on the streets immediately after committing crimes and being arrested. Democrat mayors supported the mass violence orchestrated by Black Lives Matter in nearly 220 cities in the summer of 2020, provided bail for arrested felons, defunded police forces, and instructed law enforcement to "stand down." These moves allowed protesters to loot, mug, and burn, and encouraged criminal mobs to sack and destroy downtown shopping centers and other places of business.

Democrats regard the criminal riots that took place in the summer of 2020 as social justice. The riots inflicted $7 billion in property damage and killed scores of people, which metastasized into thousands as their "Defund the Police" campaign triggered record crime waves in America's major cities. Progressives regard criminal lawlessness and mayhem as understandable responses to what they perceive as "social *in*justice"—actual courts and the law be damned. To them, mass lootings are reparations,[14] and individual robberies and thefts a socialist redistribution of wealth.

If you are in a battle of words—which is the nature of political warfare—and you are calling your enemies "liberals," portraying them as not really understanding the gravity of what they are doing, while they are calling you "white supremacists" and "Nazis," you are losing the war.

Why are Republicans so self-destructively polite? Why do they fail to see, or to *identify*, their opponents as the criminals they are, at least when they are committing crimes?

Ever since Donald Trump won the Republican Party's presidential nomination in 2016, Democrats have conducted a verbal war against white America. This war has been so effective that Gallup polls show that 61 percent of Democrats think Republicans are white racists.[15] At the same time, the Biden administration has made "equity" a centerpiece of its policies and programs.[16]

"Equity" is a weasel word used to sell a socialist agenda. The White House defines equity as privileging select racial groups with government largesse on the basis of their skin color. Such a policy is, on its face, racist, inequitable, unconstitutional, and illegal.

Even when it is the government doing the redistribution, and not street mobs, social justice—the policy of equalizing outcomes among politically select groups, regardless of merit—is another name for theft.

Redistributing income on the basis of race is not equity, it is racism. Joe Biden is the first overt racist to occupy the White House since Woodrow Wilson, who not coincidently was also a progressive Democrat. Yet, Republicans avert their eyes from this anti-American travesty. Why don't more Republicans call Democrats out for their racism?

Over the years, I gave a lot of thought to these questions, and eventually I came up with an answer that should have been obvious in the first place. The disparity in rhetorical voltage between the two political parties stems from a fundamental disparity in outlooks, and more importantly in attitudes towards the future. The left's goal is a fundamental transformation of American society.[17] Such a transformation, as I have already observed, requires a dismantling of the existing social order. To justify this destruction, the left creates narratives that provide it with ways to condemn and delegitimize the present and its defenders, and to justify its criminal agendas.

Today's left is driven by a cultural Marxist ideology, which is itself a product of the transformation of America's universities and schools into one-party training and recruitment centers for the political left.[18] A similar colonization of America's philanthropic institutions and corporate cultures has taken place, enabling this ideology to become the conventional wisdom nationally, and the strategic outlook of the Democrat Party.

Cultural Marxism, which includes Critical Race Theory, is encapsulated in the historical travesty called "The 1619 Project," inserted into the national dialogue by the *New York Times* and the Pulitzer Foundation.[19] The 1619 Project is a blatantly false narrative in which America is portrayed as having been a white supremacist, systemically racist nation since its inception, which is alleged to have taken place in 1619 rather than 1776.

Cultural Marxists regard the Constitution as a white supremacist document written by slaveowners and therefore not to be respected. Worse, according to *New York Times* editors who sponsored the 1619 Project, its purpose is to demonstrate "that nearly everything that has made America exceptional grew out of slavery."[20] This disgraceful slander against an entire people is an American version of *The Protocols of the Elders of Zion*, which is still used in many parts of the world to justify a genocide of the Jews.

From this script, it is relatively effortless for progressive activists to lift a single negative incident or atrocity from the complex history of the American Republic and frame an indictment of America's very existence. The script always leads to the same conclusion: America is a society whose institutions are systemically racist and must be first demolished, and then re-imagined according to the alarmingly vague dictates of social justice and cultural Marxism.

Conservatives approach politics from a diametrically opposed perspective. Unlike progressives, conservatives are not wedded to abstract ideologies that imagine a perfect future and use it to delegitimize an imperfect present. Conservatives seek to conserve the values of a remarkable Constitution, whose principles in actual practice have made America the world's most prosperous, most tolerant, and most egalitarian nation, and have inspired her to be a beacon of freedom throughout the world.

One consequence of conservatives' regard for the proven virtues of the U.S. Constitution and the social order it made possible is the diffidence that conservatives and Republicans exhibit in their political battles with progressives. A primary concern of the American founders was the threat of factions, whose outlooks and agendas did not encompass the well-being of the whole society but merely their own divisive interests and claims.

A main theme of America's founding documents, therefore, is the importance of compromise. The founders regarded attacks on the spirit of compromise as threats to the social order. The demonization of opponents by the Democrat Party is therefore anathema—or should be—to anyone who believes in the wisdom of the constitutional order. In other words, conservatives' instincts lead them to willfully tie their hands behind their backs in order to support the well-being of the civic whole.

The Electoral College, to take one important example, is an institution the constitutional framers envisaged as a means of forcing compromise between warring political factions. Election by the College instead of the popular vote compels contending parties to compete in states where they don't have natural majorities, and therefore need to compromise their agendas to win victories in battleground contests. But radicals who abhor compromise are determined to abolish the Electoral College, justifying its abolition by smearing it as "racist."

Other targets of their anti-compromising zeal are the filibuster and the United States Senate, which they denigrate as undemocratic. The Senate *is* undemocratic, but that's what the founders intended it to be. By giving lower-population states equal senatorial representation as with higher-population states, the founders ensured that the more-populous states would not overwhelm the less-populous ones and establish a "tyranny of the majority." America is not a democracy, it is a republic. That's what the founders created—and that's why individual freedoms have been protected, and Americans have prospered.

The federal system and decentralization of power, vital to the freedoms that Americans enjoy, are also instruments of compromise, and also abhorred by progressives who have been busily proposing legislation to federalize elections and police forces and put them in the hands of a single centralized faction. The Democrats' campaign to pack the Supreme Court and destroy the independence of the judiciary is yet another attempt to dismantle the constitutional system and consolidate power in the hands of a single faction. Their assaults on the First Amendment are equally sinister efforts to establish a one-party state.

Conservatives and Republicans are reluctant to use terms like "criminal," "racist," and "fascist" to describe Democrats whose policies are criminal, racist and fascist because to do so would threaten the constitutional principle of compromise, on which civil peace and civil freedoms depend.

Well and good, but in the current crisis, defenders of America need to find a way to develop stronger rhetoric, along with a more realistic attitude towards the enemy they are facing, if America is to survive at all. As long as conservatives continue to respect and enforce due process, as long as their indictments are concrete and specific and evidence-based, there is no danger that they will follow in the destructive path the Democrats have chosen.

The principal weapon that progressives have deployed to advance their destructive agenda is race. But in responding to their attacks, Republicans—and conservatives generally—have displayed an unsteady hand. For example, Republican leaders like Mitch McConnell have referred to slavery in leftist terms as "America's original sin." They have done this in an effort to provide a compromising view.[21] And they have often conceded that America had a regrettable racist past and wrung their hands over it.

Well and good, but to leave it at that does a grave injustice to the American reality. For there never was a moment in American history when there was not a movement of white people calling for the abolition of slavery and racism, and even willing to lay down their lives for it.

To put this history in perspective: America didn't invent slavery and accounted for less than 1 percent of the global slave trade. If slavery is anyone's original sin, it is black Africa's, where slavery existed for a thousand years before a white man ever set foot there, and it still exists today. Virtually every slave shipped to America was enslaved by black Africans and then sold to Americans and Europeans at auctions in Ghana and Benin.

America's founding fathers—Washington, Jefferson, Madison—deplored the slave system but saw no way to abolish it immediately without a war with England and the South, which they would have lost. Eventually, their heirs did fight a war to free the slaves that cost more American lives—mainly white lives—than all of America's other wars *combined*. Every black descendant of slaves in America owes his or her freedom to white Americans like Thomas Jefferson, even though Jefferson was a reluctant slaveowner, or to Abraham Lincoln and the 360,000 Union soldiers who gave their lives to free the slaves.

Is there in all of history a comparable example of one race making such a sacrifice to free another? I am unaware of one. No American, mindful of our history, should forget this record, or bury it in silence, or compromise its truth.

When America's racial past is viewed as a whole, Americans have no need to be ashamed. People alive today who demand reparations for a slavery they never experienced, should sue the Confederacy, which fought to preserve it. They should not sue the United States government, which made such enormous sacrifices to emancipate the slaves. And no American patriots should make apologies for an American past that was shaped by lovers of freedom who set a standard for ending slavery not only in America, but also in the Western Hemisphere and finally throughout the world.

For more than 60 years following the Emancipation Proclamation, America joined white Christian powers like Britain and France, who sent gunboats throughout their empires to end the global slave trade. They were opposed by brown and black potentates, mainly Muslim, who defended the institution and refused to free their human chattel.[22]

These facts have been buried by progressives who control America's cultural institutions. They have replaced them with slanders worthy of America's enemies, which underscores the enormity of the threat America faces.

The Democrats are now a national lynch mob. They have spent the last seven years in one attempt after another to destroy a president whose political signature is "America First," by libeling him and the country he loves as "white supremacist" and "systemically racist," when there is no sound basis for either charge. They have broken precedent, tradition, protocol, and the law, and violated the Constitution to hang Donald Trump and demonize his patriotic supporters as domestic terrorists and insurrectionists—traitors—all in order to advance radical policies that have destroyed America's borders, triggered record crime waves in American cities, and blown up the best economy of our lifetimes.

To defend our country against these radical destroyers, Americans need to get a firm grip on the facts of their heritage and the realities of their present. In particular, they need to understand that America never was a racist nation—even during the brief 20-year period when slavery was legal in the North, and the 76-year period when slavery was legal in the South—which is *not* the alleged "400 years of slavery" as malicious enemies of America maintain.

Slavery in America was an English implant and the extension of an African business. There were 500,000 free blacks in America on the eve of the Civil War. That is inexplicable if America was actually a white supremacist nation, as fact-defying leftists maintain. Slavery only became an issue of racial oppression when Southern slaveowners chose to defend their system in a nation dedicated to the proposition that all men are created equal by arguing that blacks were not. What was distinctly American, however, was the declaration of equality, not the racist defense of slavery by soon-to-be-defeated owners of slaves in the South.

Given the prejudices and bigotries that are endemic to human beings of all races, Americans can be proud of their racial past and its contribution to human freedom. The raw facts are these: Slavery was an inherited system, which Americans abolished in little over a generation. There never was a successful revolt by the slaves themselves. If whites had been as universally racist as leftists maintain, blacks in America would still be slaves, and not the most prosperous, most privileged and most free blacks in the world today, including all of black Africa and the West Indies.

TWO

IDEOLOGY ÜBER ALLES

Birth control itself, often denounced as a violation of natural law, is nothing more or less than the facilitation of the process of weeding out the unfit, of preventing the birth of defectives or of those who will become defectives.

MARGARET SANGER

E VERYONE SENSES THAT THE political situation that Americans find themselves in is anything but normal. Yet, the language we use to describe current conflicts is language designed to frame them in the category of politics as usual—only more so. In speaking about current conflicts, we focus on the surface issues that divide us—record inflation, off-the-charts crime waves in our urban centers, a broken border through which millions of unvetted illegal aliens are entering the country.

Sometimes we sum it up as a double standard in the justice system that treats violent leftists as "peaceful protesters" and public school parents concerned about the abuse of their children as "domestic terrorists." That juxtaposition gets us closer to the true nature of the conflict. But it is still inadequate to the gravity of the political moment, suggesting that progressives simply fail to understand the issues at hand.

But they understand those issues very well. For progressives, the issue is never the issue. The issue is always the "revolution"—the re-imagining of American society and its transformation into a future where genders are a matter of individual preference and social justice prevails. For the left, these goals are so worthy and so necessary that they justify any and all means to achieve them. Once this is understood, one can see that under the surface of the crises we face is a sinister force that poses an existential threat to our way of life—a threat far more immediate than the putative climate apocalypse.

Morality is about following rules that ensure virtuous ends. Detach the means from the ends and what you get are the totalitarian regimes that have blighted the modern era. At the root of the current American crisis is what can only be described as the moral depravity of *woke* progressives and their radical agendas.

Is this extreme? How else to describe Senator Elizabeth Warren's response to the Supreme Court's recent decision to overturn *Roe v. Wade* with a call—unopposed by her Democrat colleagues—to close the nation's 3,000 private crisis pregnancy centers, which have been created by the pro-life movement.[1]

These pregnancy centers have recently been physically attacked by violent, pro-abortion vigilantes on the left.[2] Their crime? They are specifically set up to provide advice, support, medical services, and free supplies to women who are pregnant, in difficult personal circumstances, and facing complex life decisions.

Why would Senator Warren see such facilities as a threat unless she sees herself as the leader of a death cult, whose members regard life in the womb, *in and of itself*, as a threat to its radical agenda? Why is there no condemnation of Warren by her Democrat colleagues for this cruel and inhumane proposal, which strikes at the heart of our very purpose as a biological species for existing—reproduction?

The same question could be put to progressives over their uncritical support for Planned Parenthood, an organization that was explicitly created as a eugenics project to eliminate "inferior" races, specifically African Americans.[3] Currently, Planned Parenthood receives hundreds of millions of dollars in annual subsidies from the federal government,[4] which it supplements with profits from selling the dismembered body parts of the babies it aborts.[5]

Why, one might ask, wouldn't Planned Parenthood set aside $100 million of those revenues to create a comprehensive adoption service with the intention of saving the lives of babies whose mothers might consent to that option? Especially since the number of Americans seeking to adopt unwanted babies exceeds the number of babies aborted in any given year.[6] Why indeed, unless Planned Parenthood is also a member of Warren's death cult?

What is the rationale for not providing such a service (and choice) to its pregnant clients? The answer is obvious. Doing so would undermine the foundational myth of the abortion movement—that abortion is about a woman and her body, and doesn't involve another life.

But it does. The pregnant woman is host to an unborn human being, whom her choices and actions have implanted in her womb in transit to an independent life. By denying this obvious fact, along with responsibility for all of the choices that created it, the abortion movement rejects its fundamental obligation to the most vulnerable among us.

This detachment from the reality of one's actual condition, the choices and actions that led to it, and this lack of compassion for one's innocent victims are the hallmarks of the sociopath: devoid of conscience and lacking a moral compass. These are also the common themes of progressive crusades to re-imagine the world and make it "a better place," without regard for the brutal consequences of their actions, or the suffering they cause.

OPEN BORDERS

Joe Biden won the presidential election by the thinnest of margins—0.027 percent of the votes cast.[7] On day one of his presidency, he announced the first of more than 95 executive orders, including many that were blatantly illegal and unconstitutional.[8] Their purpose? To nullify America's immigration laws and Donald Trump's reforms to secure the southern border. Biden's nullification led directly to an invasion by millions of unvetted aliens from 200 countries, smuggled into the United States by sex trafficking, drug-dealing, paramilitary, criminal cartels.

The Trump measures that Biden canceled had reduced illegal entries at the southern border to a level 80 percent lower than the levels to which Biden's policies would quickly lead.[9] One of the measures that Trump experimented with was a zero-tolerance policy for illegal crossings, which involved immediate incarceration as a prelude to deportation.[10] Because U.S. law does not permit the incarceration of minors for the crimes of their parents, this meant the temporary separation of children from their parents. The Democrats jumped on this fact to accuse Trump of "ripping babies from their mothers' arms" and putting them in cages reminiscent of Nazi concentration camps.[11]

"Let's talk about what we're talking about," an outraged Biden said about Trump's zero-tolerance policy during the presidential debates. "What happened? Parents were ripped—their kids were ripped from their arms and separated, and now they cannot find over 500 sets of those parents and those kids are alone. Nowhere to go. Nowhere to go. It's criminal. It's criminal."[12]

These attacks backfired when photos supplied by Democrats of children in the "cages" were shown to have been taken during the Obama administration. In other words, the targets of the Democrat attacks were actually remnants of an Obama administration policy that had been in force for years without protests from the same progressives who were savaging Trump. As for Trump, he was disturbed enough about the plight of the children that after two months he abandoned the zero-tolerance policy even though it would mean failing to deport some illegal adults.[13]

From the outset, Trump had made it clear that immigration should take place legally; therefore, no illegal migrants were welcome. On day one in office, Biden reversed this policy and declared the opposite, specifically inviting even unaccompanied minors to enter the country without fear that they might be turned away at the border.

Here is the twisted way Biden's head of the Department of Homeland Security, Alejandro Mayorkas, attempted to appear compassionate while encouraging children to undertake the perilous journey to an uncertain fate: "Some loving parents might send their child to traverse Mexico alone to reach the southern border—our southern border. I hope they don't undertake that perilous journey. But if they do, we will not expel that young child. We will care for that young child and unite that child with a responsible parent. That is who we are as a nation, and we can do it."[14]

By February 2021, just a month after Biden's executive order went into effect, the number of unaccompanied children in the custody of The Department of Health and Human Services had more than doubled, to 6,581. In April, the figure grew to 20,339.[15] This was nearly nine times the number of children who had been in custody under Trump in April of the previous year.[16]

The number continued to hover between 12,000 and 16,000 per month in the fall of 2021.[17] By the end of the year, as a result of Biden's invitation, the number of unaccompanied children crossing the border illegally had grown to an astronomical *243,850*.[18] Yet, despite this massive child abuse, no cries of compassion were heard from Bernie Sanders, Elizabeth Warren, the "Squad," and the Democrats generally, who had been so horrified by the former president's two-month zero-tolerance policy, affecting one-hundredth of that total for just two months.

"Humanitarian crisis" doesn't begin to do justice to the suffering inflicted on these children during their thousand-mile cartel-run treks. *The Hill* described the journey from Central America and Mexico to the United States as "one of the most dangerous trips in the world."[19] In a report documenting the conditions of migrants between 2018 and 2020, Doctors Without Borders noted that 57 percent of the illegals who were questioned had been victims of some type of violence, in addition to the harsh conditions of the route itself.[20]

Despite these facts, Biden and members of his administration, like Vice President Kamala Harris, avoided visiting the border or recommending changes in the policy.[21] They continued to deny that the crisis was a crisis, insisting instead that it was a "challenge," and continued to make statements and implement policies encouraging parents to send their children in the custody of violent human traffickers, on this dangerous, potentially life-threatening journey.[22]

The number of child rapes at the hands of the smugglers, and the number of deaths from exposure and drowning will never be known. Nor will the extent of the scourge of communicable diseases. In a March 2021 sampling of girls at one temporary shelter for migrant teenagers in San Diego, for example, nearly 10 percent tested positive for Covid-19.[23] Fourteen percent of migrant children at a facility in Carrizo Springs, Texas, likewise tested positive.[24] In May 2021, Health and Human Services reported having found more than 3,000 coronavirus cases among migrant children in Texas during the preceding 12 months.[25]

This suffering was not, of course, confined to minors. Nearly one-third of female migrants say they were sexually abused along the way, most of those having been raped.[26] In 2021 alone, the bodies of over 650 migrants who had died from exposure, drowning, and other causes were retrieved by border patrol agents.[27] That was a number dwarfed by the casualties inside the United States, where more than 100,000 people were poisoned to death by fentanyl, a principal product of the drug trade run by the Mexicans with help from the Chinese, whose sales flourished as a direct result of the Biden administration's policies.[28]

The open border created by Biden's executive orders is effectively controlled by the paramilitary Mexican cartels, which force the migrants they smuggle to incur thousands of dollars in debt, making them hostages even after their arrival. During Biden's presidency, at least four million unvetted migrants from 200 countries have crossed into the United States,[29] in the process creating a multi-billion-dollar operation for the criminal cartels.[30]

All of the human suffering caused by these actions are direct consequences of the policies instituted by the Biden Democrats, who continued to pretend—in the shameful lie of Department of Homeland Security Secretary Alejandro Mayorkas—that "the border is secure."[31] Brazen falsehoods of this cover up of an enormous magnitude of atrocities reflect the boundless contempt Democrats harbor towards everyone subject to their rule, migrants and American citizens alike. Inaction and deceit in the face of this level of human suffering is a morally depraved response to a humanitarian crisis without precedent in the nation's history. And yet, it has sparked no revolt or opposition within the Democrat Party.

For progressive Democrats, the end, in this case changing the demographics and voting patterns of the American electorate, justifies the means: sacrificing the innocent lives of unaccompanied minor children and desperate adults, lured into the nightmare of an overland "middle passage" by a president without empathy or compassion towards those whose suffering he and his administration have caused.

Burdening working- and middle-class Americans with the bill for these callous policies, while exposing them to the predations of the thousands of criminals who slip into the country undetected, is simply unconscionable. It is also, ironically, politically counter-productive. So insensitive are Democrats to the needs and lives of ordinary Hispanic Americans that they didn't foresee the actual electoral consequences of their schemes, which have alienated large segments of their (former)

Hispanic-American constituencies. A Quinnipiac University survey released in July 2022 reported that President Biden's support among Hispanics was a pathetic 19 percent.[32]

AN EPIDEMIC OF VIOLENT CRIME

The same immoral calculus lies behind the Democrats' sponsorship of the record crime waves unleashed in America's major cities following the death in police custody of fentanyl addict and career criminal George Floyd on May 25, 2020. Floyd's death—along with dozens of others—was deliberately mis-represented as a racial killing despite the fact that no evidence was ever presented that the arresting officers were motivated by racial animosity.

Indeed, one of the indicted officers was black, one Asian, and Derek Chauvin—the chief accused—was married to a "woman of color" making such a charge preposterous on its face. In a little-noted interview following the verdict, the chief prosecutor on the case, Minnesota Attorney General Keith Ellison, was asked by Sixty Minutes whether there was a racial element to the death of Floyd, who had just ingested four times the lethal dose of fentanyl prior to his encounter with the police. The attorney general's answer: "*No.* We couldn't find one. . . . We don't have any evidence that Derek Chauvin [the white officer who had pressed his knee on Floyd's neck] factored in George Floyd's race as he did what he did."[33]

Disregarding the facts in the case, the criminal organization Black Lives Matter launched a national "campaign" to punish both police and ordinary citizens for an alleged scourge of racist terror directed at innocent blacks. It was the greatest racial hoax ever perpetrated in America and led directly to the greatest eruption of civic violence on record.

The anti-law-enforcement campaign was amplified by leading Democrats—beginning with Biden and including local leaders of Democrat-run cities, often black themselves, who hurled unfounded charges of "systemic racism" against police departments across the country.

These officials further burdened local law enforcement and demoralized officers by instituting policies of no-cash bail, and releasing tens of thousands of convicted criminals from state prisons and local jails. In the process, they created a pro-crime culture that led directly to unprecedented levels of violence directed against law-abiding, vulnerable citizens, most of whom were people of color.

Abetted by a "progressive" press that suppressed video evidence of the left-wing violence, and presented the riots as "mainly peaceful,"[34] the protests created a lynch mob mentality in which verdicts preceded and eventually supplanted due process, so that President Biden announced that he was "praying for the right verdict" on the eve of the Chauvin trial in 2021, when everyone knew that a verdict of not guilty would produce more violent riots.

Amidst this officially inspired hysteria, armed career criminals resisting arrest were portrayed as victims of a savage race war against innocent black victims, while the facts that said that "victims" were generally armed and engaged in criminal acts of resisting arrest were barely mentioned in media reports. Most notoriously, Louisville resident Breonna Taylor was portrayed as a martyr "murdered in her sleep" when she was actually standing in a hallway next to her boyfriend, who was firing his gun at the police, who had arrived with a warrant for Taylor's arrest.

As a predictable result of this lynch mob hysteria, in the year of Floyd's death, the increase in the U.S. murder rate was the largest since 1905, and possibly ever, according to data from the Centers for Disease Control and Prevention. The rise in the nation's murder rate in 2020 even exceeded the 20 percent increase measured in 2001, which was driven by the terrorist attacks of 9/11.[35] In total, the anti-law-enforcement hysteria promoted by Democrats and their pro-criminal policies has resulted in nearly 5,000 additional homicides every year since 2019.[36] The overwhelming majority of these homicides were committed by blacks against other blacks.

Unleashing violent criminals on innocent, law-abiding citizens, while at the same time defaming and crippling law enforcement agencies, reflects such indecency, such callous disregard for human life and law-abiding behaviors, that it is hard to imagine a major party in a democracy supporting such efforts. Or manifesting that level of contempt for the very people whose interests the Democrats are constantly claiming to defend and champion. But that is what happened.

ABORT THE COURT AND THE CONSTITUTION

Unfortunately, in the last six years, Democrats' contempt for the lives and efforts of ordinary Americans has grown into an assault on the democratic system itself, and not just alleged abuses of that system. The Democrats' response to the Supreme Court's decision to overturn *Roe v. Wade* in spring 2022 is emblematic of their corrosive view of the Constitution as an outdated and disposable instrument when it doesn't serve their immediate purposes.

The Court's decision to reject *Roe v. Wade* was met not with legal counterarguments but with widespread calls to reverse the result, whether by legislative measures or thuggish and illegal campaigns of intimidation against the justices who argued that *Roe* had been unconstitutionally decided. These campaigns included an assassination attempt against Justice Kavanaugh, and demonstrations at the homes of other conservative justices, explicitly banned by a law that Biden's Department of Justice refused to enforce.[37]

These illegal measures were accompanied by much talk of a Democrat campaign to pack the Court with pro-*Roe* justices and turn it into an appendage of the ruling party. This "nuclear" remedy would destroy the independence of the judiciary forever, and with it the system of checks and balances that is the heart of the constitutional order that has shaped this country's legal system and defended its freedoms for over 200 years.

The Democrats' view of the constitutional order as disposable was also manifest in its years of attacks on voter ID and the general integrity of the election system through reforms that would make it more vulnerable to voter fraud.[38]

An even more sinister aspect of the Democrat Party's war on America's constitutional order has been its support for Marxist race theory, which dismisses the Constitution as a "white supremacist" document that people are bound not to respect because it is the alleged basis of the systemic racism that has oppressed black Americans from the time of their arrival in Virginia in 1619. The nomination and appointment to the Supreme Court of Ketanji Jackson Brown, a believer in

Critical Race Theory, and its contempt for the Constitution, which as a Supreme Court justice she has sworn to defend, is a measure of how dangerous this movement has become.[40]

The attack on the social contract under which Americans have lived for more than 200 years is the core of the current crisis, including the *Roe v. Wade* decision. It explains why progressives are so uninterested in the *Roe* argument itself—i.e., the actual merits of the case. It is why they are so ready to dispense with due process—with the agreement to live by a neutral set of rules and deliberative resolutions when an impasse is reached. It is why they are so ready to support mob rule and to replace reasoned argument with intimidation. Their guide is not the reasoned process on which the Constitution insists, but the pursuit by any means necessary of a "re-imagined" future, based on untested and discredited ideas.

TRUMP DERANGEMENT AND THE ONE-PARTY STATE

From this perspective, the 2016 election of Donald Trump represented an existential threat to the progressive agenda. Progressives responded with a scorched-earth resistance to a duly elected president. The resistance took the form of an unprecedented campaign of character assassination designed to delegitimize the new president, his administration, and the 63 million Americans who had voted for him. It was, in fact, a frontal assault on American democracy and the two-party system that undergirds it.

It began with a coordinated attack, spearheaded by politically corrupt intelligence agencies, to tar Trump as a colluder with the Russians—a traitor—and also a white supremacist and therefore unfit for office. The damage these lies did over the next four years to the authority of the president, and thus to the nation he headed, is incalculable. But even the exposure of these lies—which were actually the product of a collusion among the Hillary Clinton 2016 campaign, the Democratic National Committee, and the Kremlin[40]—did nothing to stem the tidal wave of slander directed at Trump and the 63 million "racists" and "deplorables" who had voted for him.

There have been four presidential impeachments in the 250-odd years since the Constitution created the procedure. Fully half of them have been directed against Trump, whose four-year term was, by any measure one of the most successful administrations in the history of the nation—attested to by the fact that he is the only incumbent president ever to receive more votes—eleven million more—in his re-election bid, than he received the first time.

Democrats even tried to impeach Trump after he left office. This effort made no sense except that the virulent hatred directed at him was not just to remove him from the White House but to bury him as a political figure—to block the 74 million Americans who had voted for him the second time from returning him to office. It was a campaign to end democracy as we know it and replace it with a one-party state.

Just before the Senate failed to convict the private citizen Trump in February 2021, Chuck Schumer publicly vowed that if the Senate to convicted Trump, as Senate Majority Leader he would hold a vote to block Trump from ever holding public office again. The legal basis for such a ban would be a questionable interpretation of the Fourteenth Amendment, which was designed to prevent leaders of the Confederacy who had engaged in an armed rebellion from holding office in the government against which they had declared war. The Democrats had no filters for their Trump hatred. They even attacked the deeply patriotic themes of his presidency: the exhortations to put "America First" and "Make America Great Again."

Senator Tim Kaine filed his own resolution not only to censure Trump but to even bar him, under the same clause in the Fourteenth Amendment, from ever holding public office again.[41] Even this was not enough for Democrats on the warpath. Thirteen House Democrats sponsored a bill that would have barred the federal government from naming any buildings or monuments after the former president and would also have prevented him from being buried at Arlington National Cemetery.[42] Representative Linda Sánchez (D-California) went a step further and introduced a "No Glory for Hate Act" that would bar Trump from receiving his federal pension, office space, and paid staff, as other former presidents have. According to the *Washington Times*, Sánchez said Trump's name should not even be permitted to appear on a park bench.[43]

When House Speaker Nancy Pelosi created a congressional committee to investigate the Capitol protest on January 6th, she appointed the Trump-hating Republican Liz Cheney as its vice chair. As a member of Congress, Cheney had supported Trump's policies 93 percent of the time.[44] But to advance her political ambitions, Cheney now described the Committee's mission in these revealing words:

"At this moment, we are confronting a domestic threat that we have never faced before. And that is a former president who is attempting to unravel the foundations of our constitutional republic. And he is aided by Republican leaders and elected officials who have made themselves willing hostages to this dangerous and irrational man."[45]

"Deranged" doesn't even begin to describe the manic disconnects of these hate tantrums, which culminated in the formation of the "U.S. House Select Committee to Investigate the January 6th Attack on the United States Capitol"—a protest described by Democrats as "an armed insurrection" to overthrow the United States government, even though no arms were found on the demonstrators, and no one among those arrested was charged with attempting to overthrow the government.

Even the most common charge against the convicted protesters—trespassing—was concocted, since the extensive videotapes provided by the Capitol security cameras showed Capitol Police willingly escorting crowds of protesters into the building. This was of a piece with the Committee's official description of itself as "bipartisan," when all nine members had voted to impeach Trump, and Speaker Pelosi had broken all precedent to deny House Minority Leader Kevin McCarthy the right to select his own representatives or to permit defense counsel to be present, and due process to be observed, as had been the case with every previous committee investigation in the nation's history.

The Democrats couldn't afford to allow a defense of those the Committee labeled as "insurrectionists" who had carried out the worst crime against their country since 9/11 or Pearl Harbor. They couldn't allow a response because the dark charade they were staging effectively consigned mainly middle-aged, law-abiding, and patriotic Americans distressed by the massive irregularities in the 2020 election to months and even years of solitary confinement.

Two of those individuals, charged with trespassing, were so depressed by the humiliating charges and conditions of their incarceration that they committed suicide.[46] A former police officer who walked into the Capitol carrying a stick he never used was convicted of carrying a stick in a "restricted building" and given a seven-year prison sentence, the kind of punishment normally reserved for those who have committed violent crimes.[47]

But the main reason dissent on the January 6 committee couldn't be tolerated was that the charge that Trump was guilty of inciting an insurrection to overturn the election was transparently farcical. In his "Stop the Steal" speech at the Ellipse, Trump had spelled out his plan for the protests. His supporters were to go "peacefully and patriotically" to the Capitol to stiffen the spines of "weak Republicans" so that they would vote to decertify the electors, as Rep. Jamie Raskin (D–Maryland) and other leading Democrats had done four years before. If Trump's followers failed to stiffen enough Republican spines, and Biden was made president, Trump told the crowd they were to go home to their districts and primary the weak Republicans in the next election so that the theft would not be repeated: "And if they don't fight, we have to primary the hell out of the ones that don't fight. You primary them. We're going to."[48]

Perfectly lawful instructions. Perfectly democratic. Period.[49]

On January 3—three days before his speech—Trump had met with the Acting Secretary of Defense and General Mark Milley in the White House to discuss security issues. According to the report of the Pentagon Inspector General, at the meeting Trump offered to provide national guard troops to protect the Capitol.

"[Acting Defense Secretary] Miller and GEN Milley met with the President at the White House at 5:30 p.m.," the IG reported. "At the end of the meeting, the President told Mr. Miller that there would be a large number of protestors on January 6, 2021, and Mr. Miller should ensure sufficient National Guard or Soldiers would be there to make sure it was a safe event. Gen Milley told us that Mr. Miller responded, 'We've got a plan and we've got it covered.'"[50] But on January 6, there were no national guards present to keep the event safe as Trump had proposed.

The most important questions the January 6th hearings were designed not to answer were these: What was the role played by the federal government in the break-in of the Capitol on that date? Was the break-in enabled by the Democrat Party to further its goals of persuading the Department of Justice to file a criminal indictment against Trump, bury him as a political figure, and tarnish the mass movement he had inspired?

A question of equal moment: How much injustice against the innocent is the Democrat Party prepared to tolerate and sanction to achieve its ends?

Four people who were present at the Capitol on January 6 died during the protest.[51] All of them were Trump supporters, and three of them died of medical emergencies. In a brazen effort worthy of Joseph Stalin himself, the Democrats attempted to portray Capitol Police Officer Brian Sicknick as a victim of the Trump mob, alleging that he was killed defending the Capitol from the "insurrectionist" mob by a blow to the head from a fire extinguisher.[52] In fact, Sicknick was an ardent *supporter* of Trump who died at home in his bed of natural causes the day *after* the Capitol protest.[53]

To put the finishing touches on this show-trial charade, the Democrats bestowed on Sicknick a rare honor by allowing him to lie in state in the Capitol Rotunda and be buried in Arlington National Cemetery. Here is how the AP reported the events (*Pravda* could not have done better):

WASHINGTON (AP) — Congressional leaders paid tribute Wednesday to slain U.S. Capitol Police Officer Brian Sicknick in the building he died defending, promising his family and his fellow officers that they will never forget his sacrifice.

Sicknick died after an insurrectionist mob stormed the U.S. Capitol on Jan. 6, interrupting the electoral count after then-President Donald Trump urged them to "fight like hell" to overturn his defeat. The U.S. Capitol Police said in a statement that Sicknick, who died the next day, was injured "while physically engaging with protesters," though the cause of his death has not been determined.[54]

Long after they were corrected, these lies were endlessly repeated by the media and the Democrats, including President Biden[55] and the January 6th Committee Chair, Democrat Bennie Thompson (D–MS).[56]

If the Democrat Party was so ruthless as to knowingly fabricate an event like this to indict people mainly guilty of trespassing, and to place them in confinement for months on end to the point where they committed suicide, what injustice would it not countenance in the service of its radical agendas?

This question was raised in the most disturbing manner by the cold-blooded murder of Ashli Babbitt, a 40-year-old Air Force veteran, and the only victim of deadly force on January 6.[57] The murder of Babbitt, who was unarmed and threatening no one, was captured on videotape along with three officers who seemed intent on not noticing the murder committed within arms-length of where they were standing.

Babbitt's killer was Capitol Police officer Michael Byrd, who had a record of recklessness with his weapon. Nancy Pelosi concealed the killer's identity for weeks on end, while she worked to see that no charges were filed against him, and then that the case would disappear.[58] The only way to describe this is that the Speaker of the House was an accomplice to Babbit's death, or murder if that charge can be sustained, as were all the members of the January 6th committee whose inquiry was ostensibly designed to get to the truth of what happened in the Capitol on that date. Not a single committee member, or Democrat generally, is on record objecting to this atrocity or seeking to get answers as to what transpired.

The Democrats are a party that has lost its way. Its moral standard is "the ends justify the means," which is no moral standard at all. In other words, it lacks a moral compass, which is why the nation that it runs lacks one, too.

THREE

WHITE SKIN PRIVILEGE

War is Peace. Freedom is Slavery.
Ignorance is Strength.

GEORGE ORWELL

ON DECEMBER 26, 1969, in Flint, Michigan, roughly 300 college students—almost exclusively white— gathered in a run-down dance hall called the Giant Ballroom. The ballroom was located in the heart of one of Flint's black neighborhoods, and also one of its most violent. A bullet hole in the front door marked the spot where, the night before, a disgruntled patron had fired a shotgun into the hall, inadvertently killing a black customer who was there to celebrate Christmas and was just in the wrong place at the wrong time.[1]

The attendees were members or alumni of Students for a Democratic Society (SDS), the largest radical movement on university campuses during the 1960s. They had come to attend the last National Council meeting of SDS.

The organization's recently elected leaders, who called themselves the "Weathermen," were billing the event as a "National *War* Council." The name was not rhetorical. Their intention was to transform SDS into an underground terrorist army whose mission was to be an "enemy within," taking up arms against America, on behalf of the non-white peoples of the world whom America allegedly oppressed. They intended to play a key role in the struggle to defeat the global empire of U.S. imperialism and replace it with a communist state.

Columbia graduate Mark Rudd, the National Secretary of SDS, described the venue of the gathering in his memoir *Underground: My Life with SDS and the Weathermen.* "The Detroit collective had decorated the ballroom unlike any other dance hall I'd ever seen. A six-foot cardboard machine gun suspended over the stage set the tone, as did psychedelic portraits of our heroes Fidel, Che, Ho Chi Minh, Lenin, Mao, Malcolm X, and Eldridge Cleaver of the Black Panthers."[2] Cleaver had earned his spot by breaking with the Panther leadership over his call for a shooting war against America, starting immediately.

The evening's speeches began with Weatherman's queen bee, Bernardine Dohrn, issuing a signature call to arms. Dohrn mounted the platform wearing a brown mini-jumpsuit and thigh-high Italian leather boots, causing a stir among the tie-dyed, blue jeaned Weather army sitting at her feet. Referring to the date on which the Weathermen had staged a three-day riot in Chicago billed as the "Days of Rage" specifically targeting police, she said, "Since October 11th, we've been wimpy."

"A lot of us," she went on, "are still honkies [radicals' derogatory term for whites], and we're scared of fighting. We have to get into armed struggle." Dohrn then began to talk about the demented killer Charlie Manson and what she referred to as the "Tate Eight"—a reference to the pregnant actress Sharon Tate, brutally murdered along with seven others, by the Manson gang, who, to emphasize their contempt, stabbed her sixteen times, stuck a fork in her pregnant belly, and scrawled "Pig" on the front door of the house they were in.[3] The deranged Manson had planned the attack, hoping to inspire a race war by blacks against whites.[4]

"Dig it!" bellowed Dohrn. "First they killed those pigs, then they ate dinner in the same room with them, they even shoved a fork into a victim's stomach! Wild!" Then she held up three fingers in a "fork salute," which immediately caught on with the crowd.[5]

Dohrn was followed to the stage by John Jacobs, known as "J.J.," a charismatic inspirer of violence and hatred directed against white "Amerikkka," as the Weathermen preferred to spell the name of their country. "We're against everything that's good and decent in honky Amerikkka," he ranted. "We will loot, and burn, and destroy. We are the incubation of your mother's nightmares."[6]

They sounded eerily like Dostoevsky's Russian revolutionaries as he portrayed them in *The Devils* (also translated as *The Possessed*): "We shall proclaim destruction—why? Why—well because the idea is so fascinating! But—we must get a little exercise. We'll have a few fires—we'll spread a few legends . . . And the whole earth will resound with the cry: 'A new and righteous law is coming.'"[7]

Next up was Rudd, who joined the nihilistic frenzy ginned up by J.J. and Dohrn. Rudd's later reflection on what he said, recorded in his memoir *Underground*, is revealing: "My own madness—possibly to keep up with that of my comrades—slipped out of my mouth as I paced the floor back and forth in front of the assembled troops. 'We have to be like Captain Ahab, we have to become monomaniacal and take the harpoon of righteousness and kill the white whale of imperialism.'"

Rudd apparently forgot that the white whale was triumphant in *Moby Dick*. Then he added: "It's a wonderful feeling to hit a pig. It must be a really wonderful feeling to kill a pig or blow up a building."[8] In recalling the speech years later, Rudd was mystified at how he could have said what he said. "Where did these words come from?" Rudd asked as though he was not their author.

He answered the question this way: "Posturing alone doesn't tell the story. They came from my righteous anger—and my grief—over what our country was doing in Vietnam and what the police were doing here at home." Rudd was a man clinging desperately to his receding humanity, succumbing to the pressure to conform to the "madness" of the moment, but then seeking to justify it.

In fact, Rudd remained permanently uneasy with the criminal, even inhuman, hatred displayed by his comrades. Dohrn's speech particularly shook him as he linked it to the extreme anti-white racism of his comrades: "There were crazy discussions at Flint over whether killing white babies was inherently revolutionary, since all white people are the enemy. Out of this bizarre thinking came Bernardine's infamous speech praising Charles Manson and his gang's murder of actress Sharon Tate. The message was that we shit on all your conventional values, you murderers of black revolutionaries and Vietnamese babies. There were no limits now to our politics of transgression."[9]

Though he recognized the "madness" he had become party to, Rudd never gave up the sanctimony of self-justification—the "righteousness" of what he thought he was doing. For revolutionaries, the end always justifies the means.

Outside the ideological bubble of the left, however, the Vietnamese Communists were ruthless aggressors and conquerors who hardly represented the Vietnamese people as a whole, while the Panthers, despite their rhetoric, had little support in the black community because they were a criminal street gang responsible for the murder of a dozen blacks and several police officers, as well as arson, extortion and rape, all of which had put them on the FBI's Most Wanted List.[10]

While Rudd never left the bubble, the doubts he was experiencing proved to be paralyzing. Because of them, he was only months away from being pushed out of the leadership of the Weathermen (the collective name of their army), and then out of the party itself.

Rudd's dilemma highlighted the problem that had led to the creation of the "Weathermen" in the first place. It explains why the National War Council of 1969 and its aftermath are so remote from the massive violent attacks that became a feature of the nation's landscape half a century later, when nearly 220 cities were attacked and torched in the wake of George Floyd's death,[11] scores were killed, and $7 billion worth of property was either damaged or destroyed.[12]

Even though the 1960s collegiate left condemned American policies in Vietnam and what they believed was America's treatment of blacks at home, white middle-class students were generally not criminals and did not have the stomach for the savage violence that revolutionary war demanded.

The problem facing the militant Weathermen was dramatized in the poor attendance at the War Council itself. The previous June, the National Council meeting had attracted 1,500 attendees, or about five times the number that showed up for the December event. The decline in support for the new militance of the organization was evidenced in the months leading up to the council. "Earlier that fall," Rudd noted, "an avalanche of chapters had disassociated themselves from the National

Office. Others had folded up, their members demoralized by the factional fighting and violence of the past year."[13]

To explain this drop-off, Rudd singled out the *Days of Rage*, the three-day riot the Weathermen leaders of SDS had staged in Chicago, which they hoped would be a test of their activists' willingness to provoke actual combat with police and had hyped as an event that would deliver a death blow to U.S. imperialism. Instead, Rudd lamented, the event had "killed SDS."[14]

The Weatherman militants had hoped to attract thousands to the battle. But only hundreds showed up willing to risk their lives and take others. Unlike the anti-police rioters fifty years later, who attracted millions to support them, inspired criminal violence that lasted for months, and produced a general crime wave in its wake, the revolutionaries of the Sixties were too middle-class, too civilized and moral to come anywhere close to matching the destructive achievements of Black Lives Matter and its followers.

Nonetheless, the core of would-be terrorists who attended the Flint War Council did go underground, concealing their comings and goings with safe houses provided by their families and supporters, forging fake identities, and disappearing into the urban wilderness, only to surface in acts of violence against police stations and policemen, and symbolic buildings like the U.S. Capitol and the Pentagon. A new leader named Billy Ayers—paramour of Bernardine Dohrn and future confidant of Barack Obama—emerged in the Underground and later wrote a memoir, *Fugitive Days*, in which he described their joy in violence: "Everything was absolutely ideal on the day I bombed the Pentagon. The sky was blue. The birds were singing. And the bastards were finally going to get what was coming to them."[15]

There were several thousand bombings in the next few years, many but not all perpetrated by the Weather Underground (as they now called themselves).[16] Fortunately, most of the bombings (but not all) targeted empty buildings, avoiding human casualties. Even the Weather Underground hit a wall when it came to the cold blooded but "righteous" murders they fantasized about.

On March 6, just over two months after the War Council, there was an explosion in a New York townhouse that leveled the building, killing three Weatherman leaders, including 23-year-old Terry Robbins, one of the most violent members of the group. The explosion was the result of three "anti-personnel" bombs they were building—dynamite packed with nails—to detonate at a dance scheduled to be held at Fort Dix for recruits and their dates. The entire Weather leadership, including Ayers, Dohrn, J.J. and Rudd, were aware of the plan and had approved it.[17]

Rudd talked to Robbins a few nights before the explosion. "Terry had told me what his group was planning. 'We're going to kill the pigs at a dance at Fort Dix,' he said."[18] But their incompetence prevented them from carrying out the plan. After the bomb exploded prematurely, killing three of the bomb-makers who were lovers and friends—the Weather Underground pulled back from the extremes toward which they were pressing, and confined most of their actions to empty buildings.

The event also precipitated Rudd's exit from the group. Eventually, he wound up a fugitive hiding in Santa Fe, New Mexico, working as a teacher and writing his memoir. In it, he remembered the months preceding the fateful War Council. "Terry and J.J., the two East Coast leaders, sure of where we were going, were providing leadership. In our many meetings in New York City, one or the other would rant, 'White people are pigs. This whole society has to be brought down. We have got to defeat white skin privilege; we can't let the Panthers and the Vietnamese bear all the costs.'"[19]

"White skin privilege," the self-justifying term that crystalized their hatred for "Amerikkka," had been picked up by Weatherman and promoted within SDS during the year of the War Council. The term was coined by an autodidact and political communist named Theodore Allen, who had written a book called *The Invention of the White Race*, and a Harvard lecturer named Noel Ignatiev.[20] It was popularized by a group of radical Harvard academics that included Ignatiev and also Cornel West, a shallow ideologue and Harvard professor known for his theatrics, which had made him famous throughout the academic world. The Harvard radicals were grouped around a magazine called *Race Traitor*, which bore the motto: "Treason to the White Race is Loyalty to Humanity."[21]

Six months before the National War Council in Flint, the *New York Times* reported that the National Office of Students for a Democratic Society (SDS) was calling "for an all-out fight against 'white skin privileges.'"[22]

The other indispensable combat term, "pigs," to describe police and military personnel, and then by extension any adversary perceived to be defending "U.S. imperialism," was inspired by the Black Panther slogan "Off the pigs!"—a direct incitement to murder cops.

A Weatherman manifesto explained:

. . . Pigs really are the issue and people will understand this, one way or another. They can have a liberal understanding that pigs are sweaty working-class barbarians who over-react and commit 'police brutality' and so shouldn't be on campus. Or they can understand pigs as the repressive imperialist State doing its job. Our job is . . . to emphasize that they are our real enemy if we fight that struggle to win. A revolution is a war; when the Movement in this country can defend itself militarily against total repression it will be part of the revolutionary war."[23]

The indispensable nature of the two derogatory terms to the revolutionary cause is obvious. You can't eliminate an enemy that you don't first demonize and hate. "White skin privilege" and "pigs" are racist poisons intended to dehumanize the enemy, erasing him in advance of the actual death blow. The intended result is that there be no counter-productive, paralyzing, guilt. The history of Weatherman shows that even if one is determined enough to dehumanize the enemy, the flesh-and-blood reality of murder makes delivering the actual death blow for people who are not naturally psychopaths or criminals difficult.

ANTI-WHITE RACISM SPREADS THROUGH THE CULTURE

As isolated as the Weathermen and the Panthers were at the time, they were still able to seed the culture and make these poisonous terms a currency in the political left. It took fifty years to grow them into a rhetoric that would permeate the culture itself—that would find currency in the White House and the ruling political party, and among the nation's intellectual elite led by the *New York Times*, underwriting an indictment of Amerikkka as a "white supremacist," "systemically racist nation," whose oppressor class is defined by its skin color.

These libels justified to millions of supporters the Black Lives Matter criminal riots, lootings, and arsons that followed the death in police custody of a delirious, high-on-fentanyl, career criminal who had resisted arrest. They also rationalized the coverup—from the White House down—of the greatest eruption of civic violence in American history as a "social justice" movement that was primarily "peaceful."

There is, in fact, no systemic racism in America that would justify the months of arsons, lootings, and shootings, and "Defund the Police" actions demanded by Black Lives Matter's criminal leaders. If there were "systemic racism" touching "every facet of American life" as Joe Biden proclaimed during his first week as president,[24] the Department of Justice would be launching massive prosecutions of police departments and other institutions for violating the Civil Rights Act of 1964, which explicitly outlaws systemic racism. There are no such prosecutions—not even in one of the eighteen thousand local police departments in this country—because there is no systemic racism in America.

There is, however, one exception: affirmative action programs in education. These received a specific exemption from the Supreme Court, which promised back in 1978 that they would be temporary. But instead of being temporary, this official discrimination not only became a permanent feature of

American life but forty years later was escalated as Biden's "equity" policy—into a massive unconstitutional redistribution of wealth on the basis of skin color.

The vehicle for spreading the poisons that underwrote both the mayhem of 2020 and the anti-white racism that has metastasized like a cancer into the mainstream culture is an educational system subverted and corrupted by anti-American radicals. In the 1970s, many of them were pursuing graduate careers in order to avoid the draft. Even so, the transformation did not happen by accident. In that decade, the most popular intellectual figure among leftwing academics was a deceased Italian Communist named Antonio Gramsci.[25] Gramsci wrestled with a problem that had burdened leftists since the First World War: Why had the Marxist proletariat failed to make a revolution? Gramsci not only came up with an answer, he proposed a solution.

According to Gramsci, the answer could be found in the fact that the capitalist ruling class exerts a cultural hegemony over society, which allows it to dominate its culturally diverse population. Through its hegemony, it is able to manipulate the culture of society as a whole—its ideas, beliefs, perceptions, and values—so that the worldview of the ruling class becomes the accepted cultural norm. The industrial proletariat is unable to overcome this disadvantage. Therefore, the revolutionary vanguard must be drawn not from the proletariat but from the intellectuals who deal in ideas, beliefs, perceptions, and values.[26]

Instead of taking over the means of industrial production as the fulcrum for transforming society, as Marx had advised, under Gramsci's plan the revolution would instead be advanced by taking over the means of *cultural* production—the universities, churches, philanthropic institutions, and media. Having achieved that goal, the radical vanguard would be able to manipulate the ideas, beliefs, perceptions, and values of the population as a whole to support its revolutionary goals.

Over the next 50 years, this set of ideas shaped a movement, which succeeded in manipulating the cultural and political institutions that shape the nation's worldview on behalf of its goal of achieving what Barack Obama called the "fundamental transformation" of the United States of America.[27] Its center was a quiet revolution in the halls of academe. By the turn of the century, there were hundreds of "whiteness studies" courses in universities across the country, taking their place alongside the ethnic and gender "studies" programs that had been launched at the end of the sixties. All these other ethnic- and gender-oriented academic fields celebrated their subjects after framing them as victims of white and male oppression. "Whiteness studies" were the exceptions. They were universally devoted to the proposition that "whiteness" was evil and needed to be abolished.

The racist perspective of the whiteness studies field was summarized by Jeff Hitchcock, executive director of the Center for the Study of White American Culture at the "Third National Conference on Whiteness," held in 1998, in these self-abasing terms: "There is no crime that whiteness has not committed against people of color. There is no crime that we have not committed even against ourselves. . . . We must blame whiteness for the continuing patterns today that deny the rights of those outside of whiteness and which damage and pervert the humanity of those of us within it."[28] A Google search today for "abolition of whiteness" yields over one million results.[29]

Mark Rudd never gave up his anti-American *animus* when he settled in Santa Fe, but he did become a teacher. When Bill Ayers retired as an unrepentant terrorist in the 1980s, he became a lecturer and then a very influential professor of education at Columbia Teachers College, where he edited a series of educational guides for K-12 schools, whose titles always began with "Teaching Social Justice" and whose tendentious texts often embraced the most unlikely subjects, like mathematics, where the pedagogy was to use body counts, in Vietnam for simple arithmetic problems.

Kathy Boudin, who was one of two terrorists to escape the townhouse that was blown up, where she was part of the bomb building team, went on to join other Weatherman alumni in the "May 19 Communist Organization," a support group for the Black Liberation Army. In October 1981, they robbed a Brinks truck, killing one guard and two officers, including the first black hired on the Nyack, New York, police force, leaving nine young children without fathers.[30]

Kathy Boudin and David Gilbert were part of the robbery team and were tried and sentenced to prison. Their son, Chesa, was raised by their comrades-in-arms, the unrepentant terrorists, Bill Ayers and Bernardine Dohrn. Chesa eventually became one of the radical prosecutors funded by George Soros to dismantle the criminal justice system. His pro-criminal policies quickly led to a record crime wave in San Francisco.[31]

Chesa's father, David Gilbert, was eventually released from jail because of his prosecutor son's efforts. His mother, Kathy, who had been tried and sentenced to twenty years in prison, was paroled early after years of effort by progressives, and in particular by the *New York Times*, which falsely portrayed her as a reformed and repentant inmate. On her release she was hired to head a program at the Columbia School of Social Work, where her faculty was entirely composed, in accordance with her wishes, of convicted felons.[32]

The most important aspect of these episodes—and there were many others like them—was the welcome these criminals received from the faculties and administrators of the schools to which they flocked. One need look no further than the "bias" in the media, the courts, the philanthropic foundations, and the Democrat Party apparatus to understand how fashionable and sympathetic a terrorist history and anti-American mentality had become in a university system that fed these same institutions and had effectively purged its conservative voices.

A study conducted in 2020 of more than 12,000 college professors from 31 states showed that professorial donations to Democrats outnumbered those to Republicans by a ratio of 95:1.[33] This would be a complete absurdity in a legitimate educational institution with no censors at the front door. A similar study of academic departments of 66 top-ranked liberal arts colleges and more than 8,000 professors showed that there were *no* Republicans on the faculties, for example, of communications departments in those schools.[34]

Communications departments are the training and credentialing institutions for members of the media. No one should be surprised, then, that the nation's media are the primary spreaders of the anti-American doctrines and hatreds of the left, including its "white skin privilege," "white supremacy" and "systemic racism" myths.

Amplifying these troubling statistics, a recent survey of 1,200 seniors by the *Harvard Crimson* revealed that only 7.1 percent of Harvard's students identified as conservatives before coming to Harvard.[35] This fact in itself indicates rampant discrimination against conservatives by the Harvard admissions office, since in a population of 330 million, roughly half of whom vote Republican, it is not possible that only 7.1 percent of blind admissions to the nation's premier school should be conservative.

Once in control of the universities, the left leveraged its cultural power by establishing "diversity" programs to indoctrinate the unenlightened into their racial world view. These required staff and eventually led to the formation of an entire highly lucrative profession of diversity trainers to take their anti-white passions into the world at large.

Across the nation, radical re-education camps are now routinely held in businesses, professional offices, medical schools, universities, and even kindergartens under the Orwellian flag of "Diversity, Equity, and Inclusion." These are thinly veiled ideological programming sessions whose message is: white people oppress black people, are inevitably racists, and are on "the wrong side of history." The hapless subjects of these sessions risk loss of face, employment, and social standing if they fail to agree with their anti-white instructors.[36]

The unrelenting purpose of these re-education classes is to instruct the unwoke in the new orthodoxy in which white skin privilege makes the world unequal and oppresses people of color by condemning them to a status absurdly described as "marginal" and "underserved." The bottom line in these self-criticism exercises is that whites need to own up to their guilt as members of the oppressor race. To deny this "fact" is a manifestation of "white fragility" and proof of guilt. Whites are privileged oppressors, regardless of their personal intentions, beliefs, behaviors, or status in life. They stand condemned as elite participants in a system that oppresses "people of color" because they are not white.

Nor should it be surprising that during the greatest eruption of civic violence in American history, the college-indoctrinated media and the Democrat Party should praise nihilistic riots and lootings as a social justice movement, while providing cover for the rioters by insisting their protests were peaceful.

Discrimination on the basis of skin color has been outlawed in America for half a century, and the equality of all its citizens has been the inspirational goal of the nation since its founding in 1776 and 1787.[37] That is why the words "white," "black," "male," and "female" do not appear in the Constitution.[38]

Given the aspiration of America's majority-white population—backed by the blood of generations—to create an inclusive egalitarian society, one might reasonably ask, "How is it possible to describe such a uniquely inspirational people as white supremacist?"

What, then, is white skin privilege? Here's my politically incorrect answer: White skin privilege is the gift of being the only racial/ethnic group in America which it is permissible—and even admirable—to single out for abuse. Indeed, handing out such abuse is obligatory for all who regard themselves as progressive, and aspire to create a brave new world of social justice.

Anti-white racism is a constant theme of the mainstream media, the popular and corporate cultures, and the educational system, from kindergarten through graduate school. It is the repetitive message of such racist shapers of public opinion as the anchors and commentators at CNN, MSNBC, ABC, NBC, and CBS, as well as the editorial boards and staffs of the

New York Times and the *Washington Post*, and their allies in the Democrat Party.

White skin privilege is the privilege of going to the back of the line for a job or promotion, a scholarship, or a place in a top-tier university.[39] It is the privilege of being presumed guilty in any controversy or conflict where a person of color is involved. In short, it is the privilege of being a second-class citizen, responsible for injustices and crimes both real and imagined, with which said citizen actually has had nothing to do, and of which he or she may be completely unaware.

White privilege is the privilege of being regarded as untrustworthy, prejudiced, and blind to the injustices one's whiteness allegedly inflicts on non-whites. White privilege is the privilege of being damned for alleged oppressions like "stop and frisk" laws, which are race-neutral, and also the often imaginary crimes of one's often merely alleged ancestors.[40]

Eighty percent or more of today's American citizens are descended from immigrants whose ancestors came to America *after* white Americans abolished black slavery, a vile institution that was all but invented in black Africa.[41] But it is a matter of social justice in today's politically correct culture to seek reparations for slavery from Americans whose ancestors never owned slaves, and were not even in the country at the time, but were oppressed themselves in ethnic and religious ghettos across the globe. Reparations for slavery are also sought from the descendants of the 360,000 mainly white Union soldiers who gave their lives to abolish slavery.[42]

In the ideological worlds of the radical left, facts are irrelevant. It's all about skin color deployed as a weapon to advance anarchistic and totalitarian agendas.

White skin privilege is the privilege of being held responsible for slavery when virtually every black slave transported to America was originally enslaved by black Africans;[43] when white America accounted for less than 4 percent of the African slave trade to the New World;[44] when the global slave trade was mainly run by Muslim "people of color";[45] when white America and England led the world in abolishing slavery, while people of color in the British empire defended it.[46] And when slavery is an institution that still exists in non-white Africa today.[47]

White skin privilege is the privilege of being scapegoated for every failure of those people of color who are unable to take advantage of the opportunities America affords to all races, and in particular to the vast majority of African Americans who have successfully made it into the working, middle, and upper classes.

America is now facing a national political crisis over its southern border because of the poverty and oppression caused by the corrupt politics and leftist economies of Central and South America, which have prompted their citizens to break into our country illegally. Conditions in the resource-rich southern hemisphere are so bad that 20 million of its residents have already broken the law to violate our sovereignty, bankrupt our social services and educational systems, and fill our jails.[48]

According to the left, to build a wall to stem this flood is "white racism"—or, as a top Democratic strategist put it recently, "Building a wall says, 'If you are brown, turn around.'"[49] Such racist logic provides an excuse for Democrats to open our borders to the world's Islamic terrorists who are also brown, and have killed hundreds of thousands of mainly brown victims since 9/11.[50]

Here is how the website "Learning for Justice" explains the invisible powers of "white privilege" to its target audience of K–12 teachers:

> It seems logical that a person should have the chance
> to prove themselves individually before they are
> judged. It's supposedly an American ideal. But it's a
> privilege often not granted to people of color—with dire
> consequences. For example, programs like New York
> City's now abandoned "Stop and Frisk" policy target
> a disproportionate number of black and Latinx [sic]
> people.[51]

Stop and Frisk was originally a New York law enforcement policy designed to make random checks for concealed weapons, and thus to prevent potential armed robberies and homicides.[52] It was instituted by conservative Republicans and subsequently ended by left-wing Democrats as "racist."[53] Like all analyses offered by progressive racists, the Learning for Justice explanation eliminates specifics like the motivations for the policies, and the details of their applications. It thus obscures from view all the actions of individuals that might account for the disproportionate number of blacks and Hispanics affected, in order to focus on the invisible but sinister oppressor, white skin privilege.

In reality, the selective nature of the policy was dictated by the fact that 98 percent of the homicides in New York City are committed by blacks and Hispanics. Blacks constitute only 23 percent of the city's population but they commit nearly 70 percent of the armed robberies, while whites are responsible for fewer than 5 percent of the same.[54] In other words, the Stop and Frisk policies that discover "disproportionately" concealed and illegal weapons among blacks and Hispanics have an explanation that is behavioral, not racial. So-called white privilege is a myth.

The stubborn fact remains that whites account for a minuscule amount of the homicides and robberies in New York City.[55] Therefore, law enforcement officials are wise to be less interested in them. On the other hand, more than 90 percent of the homicide victims of blacks and Hispanics are other blacks and Hispanics.[56] So Stop and Frisk should really be seen as a privilege for the black and Hispanic communities who are the potential targets of lethal criminal behavior, and therefore favored for protection.[57] Or it *was* a privilege until the left, led by the radical mayor of New York, ended the practice.[58]

Most examples offered by proponents of the white skin privilege scam depend on attributing all disparities among races to "systemic racism" rather than to the habits, attitudes, and actions of individuals. For example, the Learning for Justice article tells us, "the ability to accumulate wealth has long been a white privilege—a privilege created by overt, systemic racism in both the public and private sectors."[59]

Learning for Justice doesn't identify any overt racism or racist acts (which are illegal) or examine any of the individual behaviors that lead to wealth accumulation. That white racism denies blacks the opportunity to amass wealth would be news to Oprah Winfrey, daughter of a sharecropper, raised in segregated Mississippi, and now the richest woman in America with a net worth of $3.5 billion;[60] or billionaire basketball player and TV host Shaquille O'Neal; or hip hop mogul, clothing magnate, and outsize celebrity Sean "P. Diddy" Combs or ghetto survivor Snoop Dogg or any of the many blacks who have managed to accumulate tens and hundreds of millions of dollars in a single lifetime.

Seventy percent of black children in the United States are born out of wedlock, thanks in part to a welfare policy inflicted by leftists on America's poor that cuts off benefits for homes where a father is present.[61] All other factors being equal, including race, a child raised in a single-mother household is *seven times* more likely to be poor than a child raised in a household with two parents.[62] But facts like this are generally excluded from the studies that claim the wealth gap is intractable. "Inherited wealth" is often invoked as an insuperable advantage—a privilege of which allegedly only whites can take advantage. But 80 percent of all millionaires are first-generation millionaires. In other words, they earned their deserts and did so in a single generation.[63]

"White skin privilege" is not only itself a racist term, but part of a totalitarian ideology—often referred to as "identity politics"—which erases the individual in favor of group identities based on race and gender. It warps language to conceal the facts that refute its claims. "White skin privilege" is an Orwellian construct to scapegoat whites who in reality, and in alliance with minorities, have created the most tolerant and inclusive society in human history.

The term "undocumented immigrant," favored by progressives, is another form of Orwellian Doublespeak designed by leftists to suppress the fact that millions of aliens have violated the nation's laws, circumvented its citizenship process, and stolen places that belong to those applying for entry legally. It is part of the left's criminal efforts to eliminate by *fiat* the very concept of citizenship, along with the obligations it entails, in exchange for the rights and privileges it bestows.

Similarly, the term "underserved communities," universally used to justify privileges granted on the basis of skin color, suppresses the truth that these privileges are only necessary because the beneficiaries are unable to qualify under the same standards required of others. In other words, to obscure the fact that nobody is under*serving* these communities, they are underserving themselves. If there is a lack of stores and services in inner-city communities, for example, out-of-control crime rates and drug abuse are obvious reasons. But decriminalization of crimes and legalization of drugs are progressive causes!

No one in their right mind thinks that the admissions staffs at America's left-wing colleges are excluding black and brown minorities for racist reasons. Especially not when the same colleges are spending hundreds of millions of dollars to seek out and recruit minorities, while lowering their entrance requirements to benefit them in the process.[64] By ascribing every disadvantage to racism, progressives remove accountability from the so-called oppressed, and deny them the incentive to change self-destructive behaviors.

The only reason for the subterfuge "underserved" is to provide a justification for the fact that the applicants are unqualified—for whatever reasons—and in need of special privileges. By using structural categories like race to lump the qualified and the unqualified together, progressives create the fiction that minorities as a group are marginalized and excluded by whites, and incapable of meeting the same standards. What progressives really mean by this conflation is that they regard some minorities as inferior and unable to perform up to the standards of others—not only whites, but also Asians and successful blacks.

The reality is indisputably different. Far from being marginalized, blacks are the center of national attention, a dominant force in the popular culture, and the beneficiaries of government provided privileges and support unrivalled by any other ethnic group. The fact remains that 80 percent of blacks are productive citizens securely within the working, middle and even upper classes.

Today's progressive left—more accurately, today's progressively *fascist* left—has embraced a racist doctrine in which white people are scapegoats who serve a political purpose similar to the Jews of the Third Reich, though obviously not so defenseless.

In the end, the stigma of white skin privilege serves the same purpose for contemporary radicals seeking to re-imagine and transform America according to socialist designs as it did for the Weathermen, who embraced and popularized it. If America is a white supremacist nation, and has been since its inception, then by the very values of equality and tolerance that Americans cherish, America and its institutions are not worth respecting or defending. White skin privilege is a racist weapon to dismantle and destroy the nation we have known and loved, in which we have prospered until now.

FOUR

EXISTENTIAL THREAT

Our system of race is like a two-headed Hydra.
One head consists of outright racism—the
oppression of some people on grounds
of who they are. The other head consists
of white privilege—a system by which
whites help and buoy each other up.

RICHARD DELGADO, *CRITICAL RACE THEORY*

AMERICA'S SECRETARY OF DEFENSE, General Lloyd Austin is a military leader who presided over the withdrawal from Afghanistan in the summer of 2021—the worst, most incompetent, most costly, most humiliating defeat in the history of the American military.

The incompetence of the retreat, the reckless abandonment of military assets and weapons, the empowerment of the Taliban and al-Qaeda terrorists, the betrayal of America's allies in country, and the failure to consult with American allies abroad by Austin, the State Department and the military brass, were so inexplicable that they caused former British Prime Minister Tony Blair, one of America's staunchest allies, to describe the fiasco as "tragic, dangerous, unnecessary" and "imbecilic."[1]

Defense Secretary Lloyd Austin is black. He was appointed by Biden to display the wonderful diversity choices of the most progressive president in history. He wasn't chosen because he was a brilliant military leader. He was chosen because he was both black and a political hack ready and willing to embrace even the most anti-military and suicidal left-wing policies and ideas.[2]

In the opening statement he prepared for his January 2021 confirmation hearing, Austin shockingly made no mention of the upcoming withdrawal from Afghanistan, or the threats from the Taliban and al-Qaeda, whose alliance had led directly to 9/11 and was about to be revived.

Instead, the man who was now at the top of America's military chain of command vowed in author Daniel Greenfield's words, "to fight the 'enemies' that 'lie within our own ranks' and to 'rid our ranks of racists and extremists,'" by which he meant anyone who wasn't on board with Critical Race Theory and the rest of what was about to be his administration's radical leftist agendas."[3] Since becoming secretary of defense, Austin has required both Critical Race Theory—a Marxist attack on America as a white supremacist society from its beginnings to the present—and the infamous 1619 Project which conflates America with slavery—as core elements of the Pentagon's military training programs.[4]

In February 2021—with the deadline for withdrawal from Afghanistan a bare three months away[5]—General Austin was not ordering a military alert to prepare for what was going to be a major humanitarian and military reckoning. Instead, he was ordering a two-month military "stand-down" to indoctrinate America's troops in Black Lives Matter hate-white-people and hate-America propaganda.[6]

As a reality check, note that 85 percent of the troops who actually gave their lives during the 20-year war against Islamic terrorists in Afghanistan were white. These white troops died to protect the multi-racial and multi-ethnic American homeland and to give the Afghan people and especially its women the right to breathe free.[7] If America were a "white supremacist" nation, this sacrifice would be inexplicable.

Diversity, equity, and inclusion training as practiced in the military, as it is in businesses and universities across the country, is a sustained racist attack on white America. Its instructors have the hateful crude mentality of the Jim Crow bubbas of the past, only with the skin colors reversed. Their goal is to demonize *white* Americans and promote an anti-American agenda that strikes at the heart of a soldier's military oath to defend the Constitution and the nation this social contract created.

Here is a sampling of the beliefs with which our soldiers were being indoctrinated during the two-month stand-down in the run-up to the Afghanistan catastrophe:

- That the country was founded by racists.
- That the country has always been racist.
- That the Constitution's ratification codified white supremacy as the law of the land.
- That whites are inherently racists (whether they realize it or not).
- That the country must transform and become something altogether different from what it was and is.[8]

We know this is the military's diversity-training curriculum because Lt. Colonel Matt Lohmeier—a commander in the Space Force and head of a unit tasked with identifying ballistic missile launches—experienced it first-hand and had the courage to report it knowing that doing so would cost him his career. Lohmeier's love of country motivated him to tell the non-military world about the rot in the military that is eroding the confidence and patriotic dedication of its personnel. He did so in a learned, self-published book called *Irresistible Revolution* from which the quotes above are taken.[9]

For this gesture of patriotism and dissent, the Space Force removed Lohmeier from his command and summarily dismissed him from the military.[10] They then stripped him of his pension, earned during fifteen years in the armed services. From his testimony, we know that to criticize the Marxist insurrectionists of Black Lives Matter or their poisonous doctrines and lies is forbidden in today's military, as presided over by diversity commander Secretary of Defense General Lloyd Austin.

What is the impact of these doctrines on the troops? How does one honor an oath to defend a Constitution that allegedly institutionalizes white supremacy?

Lohmeier's answers:

[It] is wrecking young people's motivation to serve in the US military, regardless of their political leanings. Many of those who believe these false narratives are finding their motivation for continued service shattered. Many of those appalled by the accusations are likewise demotivated. These narratives are teeing up a lose-lose scenario for the uniformed services and for the American people. I know because I am hearing about it all the time from people at my own base and elsewhere.[11]

In October 2020, Lohmeier attended a discussion group, set up as part of the military's indoctrination program. It was led by a black female officer who assigned a book by Ijeoma Oluo called *So You Want to Talk About Race*.[12] Oluo is Nigerian and a Black Lives Matter star. Her book has been widely read and praised on the left. Here is its wisdom as Lohmeier reports it:

> The book teaches that the United States is "a white
> supremacist society" that must be "dismantled piece
> by piece." It teaches that speech that makes "people
> of color feel unsafe" is "an act of violence," but that if
> whites are uncomfortable, "do not allow [them] to be
> treated as if harm has been done to them."[13]

Could Oluo's mind-numbing and will-sapping racism be any clearer?

This racist garbage would be of little consequence if it were not the dominant theme in America's culture today, promoted by the White House, the popular culture, and corporate giants like Google and Apple, which have instituted the same racist indoctrination programs for their employees and everyone within their reach—which is everyone.

What makes these doctrines particularly sinister is that the Marxists who devised them always had the goal of dismantling America in mind. Their success in turning Afghanistan over to the Taliban, abandoning America's military bases and $85 billion in advanced weaponry, while leaving behind thousands of defenseless friends and allies in country, should be a code blue warning to every American who loves his or her country and fears for its safety.

A June 15, 2021, *New York Times* report on testimony before the Senate by Attorney General Merrick Garland and Homeland Security Secretary Alejandro Mayorkas quoted them as saying, "the greatest domestic threat facing the United States" came from what they both called "racially or ethnically motivated violent extremists, . . . specifically those who advocate for the superiority of the white race."[14]

And where are these white domestic terrorists exactly? Where are their arguments for white superiority? Where are their outrages? An Internet check of "white supremacist attacks" turns up virtually nothing—so isolated and uncoordinated are the few lone wolf incidents that have taken place. Any American with open eyes knows that the opposite is nearer the truth. Anti-white racism and ignorant attacks on the American founding are more accurately seen as an existential threat to Americans and our country. There are more than half a million interracial crimes of violence between blacks and whites annually. Ninety percent of them involve violent crimes by blacks against whites.[15] And why not, given the popularity of anti-white racist lies in the mainstream media and the political culture?

PELOSI'S TERRORIST CAUCUS

Congresswoman Ilhan Omar is a leader of the House caucus known as "The Squad," which includes such like-minded, anti-American radicals as Rashida Tlaib, Alexandria Ocasio-Cortez, Ayanna Pressley, and Cori Bush.

Omar is a refugee from Somalia, where she grew up in a family that was part of the Somali elite. Omar's father and grandfather worked for the despotic regime. Her father, Mohamed Nur, was a communist, who served as a propagandist for the Somali dictator Siad Barre. Under Siad Barre's rule, Somalia had become a self-styled Marxist-Leninist client of the Soviet Union.

Barre's dictatorship was characterized by the United Nations Development Program in these chilling terms: "The

21-year regime of Siad Barre had one of the worst human rights records in Africa."[16] A Human Rights Watch report titled *Somalia: A Government at War with its Own People* estimates that in one year, the regime killed between 50,000 and 60,000 people.[17] An Amnesty International report describes the official methods of torture in these words: "beatings while tied in a contorted position, electric shocks, rape of women prisoners, simulated executions and death threats."[18]

Ilhan Omar's family—now refugees in the United States—served this nightmare regime through all its violence and violation of human rights, but to this day she has not offered a statement of regret about their service to this carnage.

When Omar was nine years old, the Barre regime was toppled in a civil war, and Omar's family fled to a Kenyan refugee center along with other Somalis complicit in its crimes. They remained there for four years, until they were admitted to America despite fraudulent claims they had made to immigration officials, which normally would have barred their entry. To enable his entry, Omar married her brother, a fact she concealed, while her father remained a communist, which he also concealed.[19]

From the beginning of her career as a political activist, Omar's chief connections and financial support have come from a network of jihad-supporting Muslim Brotherhood fronts, and pro-Iranian terrorist groups—Hamas, Council on American–Islamic Relations (CAIR), and American Muslims for Palestine, to name a prominent few.[20] She has returned their favors by standing up for Islamic terrorists and blaming their violent actions on America.

At the very outset of her public career as a member of the Minneapolis City Council, Omar caused a stir by making a public plea for leniency on behalf of several Somali refugees whom she conceded were her "friends," who had been arrested while seeking to join the violent Somali terror group al-Shabab. The al-Shabab terrorists formally pledged their allegiance to al-Qaeda and its leader Ayman al-Zawahiri.[21]

It was the nature of Omar's plea in their behalf, however, that was most disturbing. "They were happy young men," she said. "And then at some point, something happened. And that is what needs to be researched and studied. What is happening to make them feel disconnected from a community that has birthed them, that has nurtured them?"[22]

Omar had the answer. What drove people to become terrorists was America and Donald Trump: "Our president [Trump] is their [jihadis'] best PR person. . . . It's a perfect selling and promotional tool. The president says, 'We are at war with Islam. We are at war with people who come from countries that are majority-Muslim countries. And we favor the people in those countries who are not Muslim.' What more do you need?"[23] Actually, it was Osama bin Laden in 1998, a year Bill Clinton was president, who issued a formal declaration of war against "the Jews and Crusaders" (Christians) that is still in progress today.

Omar was elected to Congress in 2018 with the full support of the Democrat Party leadership to fill former Democratic National Committee chair Keith Ellison's congressional seat. She received 80 percent of the vote. Given the backing of the Somali community, this was hardly a surprise, since the Minneapolis suburb she represented had an estimated 100,000 individuals of Somali heritage—the largest such community in the United States.[24]

Just before Omar's election, President Trump had issued an executive order imposing a moratorium on migration to the U.S. from six majority-Muslim nations that were considered failed states in which terrorists were so influential that the vetting process for migrants could not be trusted. Allowing immigration from these countries was regarded as an unacceptable risk. This measure seemed uncontroversial because immigration from the same six countries had been blocked by the Obama administration due to of the same security concerns. Trump was merely extending the order. But Democrats ignored the facts and insisted on calling it Trump's "racist ban" on Muslims.

Omar led the local resistance to Trump's executive order, saying, "This ban on refugees is rooted in racism and Islamophobia."[25] It was, in fact, her signature explanation for every effort to oppose Islamic terrorism and defend the United States. On her election to Congress, Omar was interviewed by Al Jazeera TV. The interviewer asked her how she would respond to conservatives who said that the rise in so-called Islamophobia is "a result not of hate, but of fear, and legitimate fear, they say, of quote-unquote, 'Jihadist terrorism.'"

Omar's revealing answer was this: "I would say our country should be more fearful of white men across our country because they are actually causing most of the deaths within this country. And so, if fear was the driving force of policies to keep America safe—Americans safe inside this country—we should be profiling, monitoring, and creating policies to fight the radicalization of white men."[26]

The idea that white men are causing most of the deaths within this country is so preposterous and so riddled with racial hate that even to cite a statistic to refute it—and there are many—would be a distraction from what Omar reveals about herself; that she is a rabidly anti-white, anti-American racist whose loyalties lie with America's most violent and barbaric enemies.

Despite these views, four months after Omar's election to Congress, Speaker Nancy Pelosi appointed her to sit on the House Foreign Affairs Committee, where she was given access to the nation's most classified secrets. Her prestigious committee assignment also provided her with a platform that she used to become the chief defender of America's Middle East enemy, Iran, a terrorist theocracy that has threatened the assassination of American presidents and cabinet members—including former Secretary of State Mike Pompeo—and is responsible for thousands of American casualties and deaths in Lebanon and Iraq.

Encouraged by Pelosi's support, Omar continued to display her malicious attitude toward the country that had rescued her and her family and lifted her to the heights of political power. In the course of a keynote speech she gave at a CAIR fundraiser in March 2019, she portrayed the unprecedented and unprovoked 9/11 attacks that took the lives of over 3,000 American civilians, and were therefore war crimes, as nothing very serious. Then, she summed up 9/11 as an unprovoked attack on Muslims, to whom she alleged Americans denied civil liberties.

Her speech began with a completely false statement describing 9/11 as the event that inspired the creation of CAIR. In fact, CAIR was founded in 1994—seven years before the attacks. It was created by Muslim Brotherhood and Hamas leaders, which linked it to a global terrorist network for whom it provides precisely the kind of "nobody here but us victims" propaganda that Omar's speech exemplified.[27]

In Omar's own inflammatory words that evening: "CAIR was founded after 9/11 because they recognized that some people did something and that all of us were starting to lose access to our civil liberties." Omar said in the same speech, "But no matter how much we have tried to be the best neighbor, people have always worked on finding a way to not allow for every single civil liberty to be extended to us."[28]

Some people did something—quite the way to characterize one of the most traumatic events in the history of the nation. To that she added the insult that it was properly seen as an attack on *Muslims*—five hundred million of whom, according to polls conducted by Al Jazeera and other Islamic sources, actually approved of the 9/11 attacks and its war crimes against American civilians.

While there were isolated post-9/11 incidents of vigilante attacks—one on a Sikh, who was not a Muslim, President Bush went out of his way to distance Islam from responsibility for the atrocity: "The face of terrorism is not the true faith of Islam," Bush said, as though he were an Islamic authority himself. "That's not what Islam is all about. Islam is peace."[29]

In reality, Americans responded to the heinous 9/11 attacks with admirable restraint. There were no orchestrated anti-Muslim pogroms in the wake of the atrocity, and the Bush administration even flew the bin Laden family and a planeload of Saudis who might have been implicated in the attack to safety in Saudi Arabia.

The idea that Muslims are the chief targets of religious persecution in America is a Muslim Brotherhood myth. The religious group that according to the FBI statistics is the target of the most religious hate crimes is Jews—and by a wide margin, and frequently at the hands of Muslims. According to the FBI, American Jews are *five times* more likely than Muslims to be the victims of religious hate crimes[30]—many of which have been incited by the poisonous anti-Israel propaganda spread by pro-Islamist groups like the Muslim Students Association, American Muslims for Palestine, Students for Justice in Palestine, and the Boycott, Divestment, and Sanctions movement—all of which are supporters of terrorist causes supported by Congresswoman Omar herself.[31]

Omar's hatred for the Jews had made her notorious even before her election to Congress, as she supported Hamas's war crimes against Israel each time Hamas launched thousands of rocket attacks targeting Israeli civilians from the Gaza Strip. In support of the unprovoked 2012 attacks, Omar tweeted: "Israel has hypnotized the world, may Allah awaken the people and help them see the evil doings of Israel." [32]

When Omar's anti-Semitic, pro-terrorist efforts finally generated a firestorm of outrage and calls by Republican leaders for Nancy Pelosi to remove Omar from the House Foreign Affairs Committee and bar her from intelligence briefings, fellow Squad member Rashida Tlaib sprang to her defense. "I am tired of colleagues (both D+R) demonizing @IlhanMN," Tlaib said on Twitter. "Their obsession with policing her is sick. She has the courage to call out human rights abuses no matter who is responsible. That's better than colleagues who look away if it serves their politics."[33]

Typically, this statement is a brazen lie, since neither Omar nor Tlaib herself has ever had the integrity to call out Hamas or Iranian terrorists for their unprovoked attacks and war crimes against the Jews. Both Omar and Tlaib have supported those attacks.

Tlaib and fellow Squad member Alexandria Ocasio-Cortez headlined a fundraising event for "American Muslims for Palestine" in April 2019.[34] AMP is an organization created and controlled by Hamas, which is officially committed to a genocide of the Jews, and also funds the Jew-hatred campaigns of Students for Justice in Palestine on American campuses, spearheading the terrorist-backed Boycott, Divestment, and Sanctions movement that seeks to strangle the Jewish state.[35] Tlaib, Ocasio Cortez, and all the members of the Squad are unapologetic supporters of the terrorist regimes on the West Bank and in Gaza.

In defending the genocidal Palestinian campaign to rid the Middle East of Jews, Tlaib invented the following history: "There's always kind of a calming feeling, I tell folks, when I think of the Holocaust, and the tragedy of the Holocaust, and the fact that it was my ancestors—Palestinians—who lost their land and some lost their lives, their livelihood, their human dignity, their existence in many ways, have been wiped out, and some people's passports, and, just all of it was in the name of trying to create a safe haven for Jews, post-the Holocaust, post-the tragedy and the horrific persecution of Jews across the world at that time, and I love the fact that it was my ancestors that provided that, right, in many ways, but they did it in a way that took their human dignity away and it was forced on them."[36]

One would be hard pressed to find a series of more outrageous lies. In fact, the Muslim Brotherhood's campaign to wipe out the Jews of the Middle East was a pro-Nazi campaign from its beginnings. The Muslim Brotherhood translated Hitler's *Mein Kampf* into Arabic in the thirties. The spiritual leader of the Brotherhood's campaign to "push the Jews into the sea" is Haj Amin al-Husseini, considered the father of Palestinian nationalism.[37]

Al-Husseini, whose title was "Grand Mufti of Jerusalem," was an admirer of Hitler and spent World War II in Berlin recruiting an Arab legion to fight for the Nazis. A Jew-hating Nazi himself, he drew up plans to build an Auschwitz in the Middle East, which was only thwarted when Montgomery defeated Rommel at El Alamein.

A dedicated jihad activist, Congresswoman Tlaib has headlined fundraisers for the Hamas spin-off "American Muslims for Palestine."[38] She is a fervent supporter of the terrorist regimes on the West Bank and in Gaza, as are the other members of the so-called congressional "Squad," which is, in effect, a terrorist caucus in the Democrat-run House.

The Hamas-controlled American Muslims for Palestine is one of the founders of the recently formed U.S. Coalition of Muslim Organizations.[39] This is an Islamist coalition composed of the leading Muslim Brotherhood groups in America. The purpose of the Coalition is to conflate all Muslims with the Islamists—the Muslim supporters of the terrorist *jihad*.

Shortly after its formation, the Coalition hosted a "Muslim Advocacy Day,"[40] which was attended by Omar, Tlaib, and fellow "Squad" member and ally Alexandria Ocasio-Cortez, who is not a Muslim but an activist in the Islamist-Progressive Alliance—an alliance whose members are united in their hatred of the Jewish state and their solidarity with Palestinian terrorists.

The hatred of Tlaib and Omar for Israel's Jews is so encompassing and intense that they led the opposition by nine members of the House to an Israeli request for congressional funding of the Iron Dome missile defense system, which is all that stands between Israeli civilians in Tel Aviv and other cities and the thousands of Iranian rockets supplied to Hamas terrorists who target civilians in total disregard of the Geneva Convention.[41]

The Coalition of Muslim Organizations' goal of conflating all Muslims with Muslim supporters of the terrorist jihad is the other side of the equation demonizing all white people as racists. It provides cover for the terrorists, who are now seen as harmless "victims" and therefore incapable of committing war crimes and genocidal acts.

This "unholy alliance" between American radicals and Islamic terrorists—as I described it in a book by that name published sixteen years ago—now includes the leadership of the Democrat Party.[42] When President Trump responded to Omar's slurs characterizing 9/11 as an attack on Muslims with a tweet saying, "We will never forget," House Speaker Pelosi circled the wagons around the offender, claiming that Omar was the victim of a racist attack, and implying that the president was inciting a lynch mob against her, because she was a black member of a religious minority.[43]

In a response to Trump's "We will never forget" comment, Senator Bernie Sanders wrote: "Ilhan Omar is a leader with strength and courage. She won't back down to Trump's racism and hate, and neither will we. The disgusting and dangerous attacks against her must end."[44] This inversion of the facts fooled only the uninformed and the progressive faithful.

Pledges of solidarity with supporters of Jew-hating terror-ists were echoed in statements from all the leading Democrat candidates for president, who elevated Trump's comment into an incitement to violence against Omar because she was a Muslim and black. In the malicious formulation of Senator Elizabeth Warren: "The President is inciting violence against a sitting Congresswoman—and an entire group of Americans based on their religion. It's disgusting. It's shameful. And any elected leader who refuses to condemn it shares responsibil-ity for it."[45] What are disgusting are these smears targeting supporters of the Jews of Israel who are victims of a 70-year unprovoked terrorist war of aggression against the Jewish state, whose genocidal goal, as articulated by the terrorist head of the Palestinian Authority, Mahmoud Abbas, is to render a "liberated" Palestine *Judenrein*—Jew-free.[46]

As of this writing, there have been over 40,000 deadly terror attacks by Muslims since 9/11, carried out against Christians, Jews, Yazidis, Hindus, Buddhists, and other "infidels," which have resulted in hundreds of thousands of deaths.[47] Democrats and progressives seem to think this slaughter of innocents in the name of Allah is not actually the work of Muslims but rather of impostors who have hijacked the Muslim faith while not actually believing its tenets. They cling to this fantasy even though the Qur'an instructs its followers to "slay the infidels wherever you find them"[48] and specifically prescribes behead-ing them—"strike them in the neck."[49]

Progressives persist in this self-delusion even though the Muslim Brotherhood, al-Qaeda, ISIS, Hamas, and other terrorist groups are guided by leading Muslim scholars like Sheik Yousuf Al-Qaradawi, spiritual leader of the Muslim

Brotherhood, who claims the Holocaust was God's punishment of the Jews for their corruption, and will be repeated, "next time, Allah willing, . . . at the hands of the believers."[50]

Unwilling to distinguish between peaceful Muslims and Muslim supporters of Islam's holy war, whose goal is global Islamic supremacy, progressives like Sanders, Warren, and Pelosi conflate the Islamic terror networks with all Muslims. In doing so, they serve the ends of the Muslim Brotherhood and the *jihadists*, who are self-declared mortal enemies of America and the West, turning them into victims deserving sympathy.

Contrast this attitude with the sentiments of Qanta Ahmed, a Muslim member of the Council on Foreign Relations:

Rep. Ilhan Omar continues to be an embarrassment and a disgrace for me and other American Muslims with her outrageous, ignorant, anti-Semitic and now anti-American comments. While Omar, a Minnesota Democrat, holds herself out as a proud Muslim, she repeatedly projects a distorted and patently Islamist interpretation of Islam—a religion that in reality stands for the values of justice, peace and ethical conduct.[51]

As for Omar's remarks on 9/11, Qanta Ahmed said: "Omar should be honest. There is no escaping the fact that the atrocities of 9/11 were not simply committed by 'some people.' Islamist jihadists were responsible and they came from within the Muslim fold. . . . Living at the time in the Saudi Kingdom—the epicenter of Islam—as the world learned the identity of the 9/11 terrorists, I wondered how my religion had been hijacked by suicidal killers who claimed they had a religious duty to kill innocents. And I knew from that moment that these murderers would now become the face of Islam for many non-Muslims who know little about a religion with more than 1.6 billion followers around the globe."[52]

The willful blindness of the Democrat Party leadership, and of progressive ideologues generally, is the greatest liability America faces in the global war that Islamic supremacists have declared on America and the West. What Ilhan Omar has exposed is the extent to which the Islamists and their secular allies have now infiltrated and seduced America's ruling political party. This can only have a crippling effect on the nation's efforts to defend itself.

When then-Republican Minority Leader Kevin McCarthy threatened to force congressional action against Omar and Rashida Tlaib for their anti-Semitic defenses of Palestinian terrorists, Omar explained McCarthy's motivation with an even more inflammatory charge: "It's all about the Benjamins, baby," she said, a rap culture reference to the portrait of Benjamin Franklin on hundred-dollar bills. When an editor at *The Forward* asked who Omar thinks is paying American politicians to be pro-Israel, she responded, "AIPAC!" referring to the American Israel Public Affairs Committee, the United States' most prominent pro-Israel lobby.[53]

Initially, this flagrantly anti-Semitic remark seemed a bridge too far for Pelosi and the leaders of the Democrat Party which, in the words of the *New York Times*, rebuked Omar and called on her to apologize for her "use of anti-Semitic tropes and prejudicial accusations about Israel's supporters."[54]

But when push came to shove, Pelosi backed off to the point of saying that Omar's remark had not been not anti-Semitic but a language misunderstanding—by someone who had spoken English in America for more than twenty years. As *The New York Times* reported the events leading up to Pelosi's caving: "Alexandria Ocasio-Cortez, Democrat of New York, and liberal groups like Justice Democrats and IfNotNow, accuse Democratic leaders of singling out a woman of color. . . . And there is a rising backlash from the Left on social media, where a slew of left-leaning journalists and activists are posting under the hashtag #IStandWithIlhan."[55]

"The day before the House resolution came to the floor," writes Benjamin Weingarten, the author of the book *American Ingrate*, "the Congressional Black Caucus emerged from a meeting with Omar, reportedly forming a circle around her. Representative Marcia Fudge stiff-armed reporters, protecting Omar from questioning. Then, several members proceeded to hug her." Commented the same author: "This would prove to be a metaphor for the party itself."[56]

Omar was not singled out by name in the Democrats' congressional resolution, which condemned racial prejudice, nor was the resolution focused on anti-Semitism, despite the fact that Omar's anti-Semitic attacks had precipitated it. A letter to Pelosi signed by Women's March leader and Hamas supporter Linda Sarsour and more than 600 left-wing activists claimed that criticisms of Omar's anti-Semitism were "rooted in both racism and Islamophobia." The resolution called on Pelosi to condemn "anti-Black racism and xenophobia."[57]

IDEOLOGICAL RACISM

The racism embraced by the progressive left and the Democrat Party, while as malicious, bigoted, and demonizing as the racism of groups like the Nazis and the Ku Klux Klan, is none-theless different. It is different in ways that enlarge the scope of its destructive agendas and make it a threat not just to the group it stigmatizes but to the society as a whole.

Omar's current husband, for example, is white, a miscege-nation not possible between a Klan member and a black. On the other hand, the condemnation of all whites on the basis of their skin color is the same. "White identity is inherently racist; white people do not exist outside the system of white supremacy," according to Robin DiAngelo, one of the lead-ing "diversity, equity, and inclusion" trainers and best-selling author of *White Fragility*. DiAngelo's characterization is stan-dard for the so-called diversity industry.

On the other side of the equation, by erasing individu-als—their attitudes, intentions, and achievements—the new "intersectional" racists convert all non-whites and non-males into victims, who can't be held accountable for their actions and fictions. In the words of Ilhan Omar, a particularly aggres-sive anti-Semite, "I think I know a little bit about discrimina-tion. I face it every single day. I carry multiple identities that are constantly, constantly being discriminated against."[58]

Omar stated this on the floor of the Minnesota House, well before she became a congresswoman. She said it in the course of *opposing* a resolution to condemn a terrorist-spon-sored boycott of Israel. Her rationale? The terrorist claim that Israel is an "apartheid," state, oppressing Arab Muslims. In fact, Israel's Arab Muslims have more rights and freedoms as Israeli citizens than the inhabitants of any Arab or Muslim state. Israel is the only non-apartheid state in the Middle East. Under the Palestinian Authority, for example, the sale of land to a Jew is punishable by death.[59]

Omar and her supporters use their "marginalized identities" to create a veneer of virtue around their end goal, which is to destroy the Jewish state and impose a leftist ideology on Americans. As Ibram X. Kendi, another leader of the movement, has defined its binary universe in his best-selling book *How to Be an Anti-Racist*: "There is no such thing as a not-racist idea, only racist ideas and anti-racist ideas." In other words: Agree with us or you're a racist.[60] This is the ideological prescription for a totalitarian state, and it is the dominant creed of American progressives today.

The instrumental character of the new racism makes it a weapon not just against individuals but against America's social order itself, and its grounding in *individual* accountability and freedom. By focusing on structures and group abstractions like races, genders, and classes, and undefined terms like "marginalized" and "oppressed," progressivism deflects attention from the real world and its complexities, in favor of its own invented one, a fictional melodrama it can manipulate to its own ends.

Omar's critical biographer, Benjamin Weingarten, describes the result:

> Omar's 5th Congressional District has long been led at the national, state, and local levels by progressives. How have its residents fared? Rep. Omar's district was recently rated as the worst for black Americans in the nation, on the basis of numerous socioeconomic criteria. The report noted that "Black area residents are about four times more likely to live below the poverty line than white residents and three times more likely to be unemployed."[61]

FIVE

A TSUNAMI OF HATE

Trump Derangement Syndrome (TDS) is
a mental condition in which a person has
been driven effectively insane due to
their dislike of Donald Trump, to the point
at which they will abandon all logic and reason.

URBAN DICTIONARY

ANALYSTS OF THE CURRENT crisis generally attribute it to the fact that our politics has become "divisive." They talk about "unity and healing" as those things would miraculously be achieved if everybody were to stop. . . . What? Disagreeing? All politics involves divisions. That's the healthy basis of our constitutional order: the freedom to disagree, and the protection of those with views that dissent from the mainstream.

To suppress disagreement, to outlaw it—as many on the left are demanding and implementing these days—is to end democracy as we know it. The left has even made a crusade out of attacking those who questioned the 2020 election, calling them a threat to democracy—even though Democrats themselves have challenged every presidential election that Republicans have won since 1980.

But the problem is not that we disagree. We are not suffering as a nation from differences of opinion, which the Constitution protects. The problem lies in the depths to which those disagreements have descended since the 2016 election campaign when Hillary Clinton and a cabal of intelligence officials decided that Trump must not be president under any circumstances, and that every means necessary, including illegal means like fake FISA warrants and fake incriminating dossiers, prepared with the help of the Russians, should be used to stop him.

Once Trump won, the campaign against him metastasized into a permanent impeachment effort lasting the length of his presidency and even beyond, to prevent him from ever running again. In 2020, Trump won the support of 74 million Americans—more than any incumbent presidential candidate before him. Their anti-Trump vendetta transformed the divisions splitting the country into a cold civil war.

The anti-Trump vendetta drew their strength from a tsunami of hate that falsely portrayed him as a "white nationalist," a "white supremacist," a "colluder with the Russians" (i.e., a traitor), and eventually an "insurrectionist" intending to overturn the 2020 election result by force and violence.

None of these claims had any substance. Trump had a long career as a public figure before 2016, during which he was a donor and friend to liberal political icons like the Clintons, who attended his wedding. In those pre-candidacy years, Trump and Rosa Parks together received an NAACP award presented by Muhammad Ali. During those pre-political years, he had two hit TV shows, and no reputable Democrat or commentator ever referred to him as a "white supremacist" or "white nationalist." Those slanders only began when he decided to run as a Republican against Hillary Clinton in 2016.

The insurrectionist charge is equally empty, since as previously noted, prior to January 6, Trump had offered to authorize 10,000 national guardsmen to defend the Capitol in case any trouble should occur. The Democrats in charge of the Capitol rejected his offer.

The source of the divisiveness that has made dialogue, compromise, and bi-partisanship virtually impossible is a tsunami of hate, emanating from the progressive left, the Democrat Party, and its kept media. If you demonize, criminalize, and seek to extinguish dissent by a president backed by 74 million voters, and characterize them as "racists," "sexists," "homophobes," "Islamophobes," and "deplorables," as candidate Hillary Clinton did—if you regard them as oppressive yahoos not worthy of basic respect—you have overwhelmed the kind of division that a democracy can tolerate.

A democracy can't survive if this is the attitude of a party that controls all three branches of government, is enabled by an ideologically corrupt and compliant media and is determined not just to defeat, but to humiliate, destroy, and erase a leader supported by roughly half the population. That is the heart of the problem.

These campaigns are not merely a war to cancel Donald Trump. If they were, they would be reprehensible but not a threat to the nation itself. But this hate for Trump is also hate for the 74 million Americans who voted for him. And there is no shortage of reminders of that. Ordinary Americans in all walks of life who happen to think that Trump's presidency, which included record employment and record economic growth, delivered benefits for all Americans, particularly American minorities,[1] secured America's borders,[2] defeated America's terrorist enemies, and led to an unprecedented reconciliation between Arab nations and the State of Israel,[3] was a worthy achievement. If they are treated as social pariahs, have their careers destroyed, and are regarded as mentally unfit and, in the words of Representative Alexandria Ocasio-Cortez, in need of "deprogramming," the democratic dialogue has ended.[4]

In a March 2020 interview with *Axios*, Representative James Clyburn—the third-ranking Democrat in the House and the political figure most responsible for Biden's primary victory—even raised the specter of Hitler when speaking about Trump, calling the president a racist and likening modern-day America to Germany during the Nazi Party's rise to power. "I used to wonder how could the people of Germany allow Hitler to exist," said Clyburn. "But with each passing day, I'm beginning to understand how. And that's why I'm trying to sound the alarm."[5]

SAM HARRIS'S TRUMP DERANGEMENT

In measuring the intensity of the anti-Trump fever and assessing its implications, perhaps no individual case is more instructive than that of Sam Harris, a well-known philosopher and political commentator and the author of many books, including *The End of Faith* and *The Moral Landscape: How Science Can Determine Human Values*.[6] In the latter book, he attempts to provide a "science of morality" to replace the moral relativism of atheists and the God-based morality of the religious believers.

Harris, then, is a rationalist. He is also generally a measured thinker, and in these divisive times an often independent one. In listening to the controlled, dispassionate tones of his podcast commentaries, his audiences can readily believe they are listening to the voice of reason itself. And so, on many occasions, they are—a voice balanced, thoughtful, and ready to weigh differing sides fairly.

But when it comes to Trump, Harris turns into another human being entirely. "Trump is a racist asshole;" "The worst president in human history;" "He lies more than any person has ever lied in human history; and not only does he get away with it . . . his supporters seem to delight in his running roughshod over any expectation that a public figure would be honest;"[7] (this from a supporter of Joe Biden!) "Osama bin Laden, as a person, is far more understandable to me and far less reprehensible, personally, psychologically, than Trump."[8]

Here is how Harris reads the evidence against Trump:

Whatever the scope of Joe Biden's corruption is, if we can just go down that rabbit hole endlessly and understand that he's getting kickbacks from Hunter Biden's deals in Ukraine, or wherever else, or China, it is infinitesimal compared to the corruption we know Trump is involved in.

Really? Biden's corruption entails millions of covert dollars he received from America's enemies—the Chinese and Russian communist parties—in return for what influence exactly on American policy? Biden won't say, and Harris doesn't care. "It's like a firefly to the sun," Harris offers as a comparative measure. "It doesn't even stack up against Trump University, right? Trump University as a story is worse than anything that can be in Hunter Biden's laptop."[9]

This is a mind-boggling statement. The laptop contents point to the possibility of treason by an American president and may affect such massive national tragedies as the abandonment of Afghanistan to the Chinese and the Taliban.

By contrast, Trump University was a business venture Trump was engaged in when he was a private citizen before he became president. He was successfully sued by students who claimed they had paid for something that wasn't what it had been presented to be; e.g., it was not an actual university, and Trump did not make the in-person appearances they had been led to expect. Trump protested but paid a $25 million settlement.[10] Case closed.

Hunter Biden's laptop contains a record of the money deals he made with America's communist enemies while his father was in the White House, and with his father's knowledge. Hunter complained that he had to kick back much of his gains to "the Big Guy." The deals involved millions of dollars received by the Bidens in exchange for influence in the White House. Fifty-one top intelligence officials, including heads of the CIA and DNI, signed a false statement declaring the laptop "Russian disinformation" in order to elect his complicit father to the presidency. They did so knowing full well that the laptop was authentic. It is far more likely that Trump's misdeeds are the "firefly" to the Bidens' sun.

Before getting into the details of Harris's attitude toward the Bidens and, more importantly, its implications for America's future, it is worth pausing to appreciate just how independent a thinker on the left Harris is—how willing to defend a perspective that is anathema to his political allies.

Right after Harris's comment that Trump is a "racist asshole," he makes this observation:

But fully half of the allegations that I've seen about him being racist made in public seem totally spurious, and that's a huge problem. And it's totally inconvenient to have to make that argument, because again, I think he's the worst president in human history. And anything that can be made to stick against him should stick because he's an existential threat to our democracy.

But take the case that is often made against him, where in the aftermath of Charlottesville, he said there were "fine people" on both sides and in that moment couldn't even condemn white supremacists. Rather, he referred to them as "fine people." This allegation is just ubiquitous against him on the left, that every journalist makes it, Joe Biden makes it, Kamala Harris makes it. They're never criticized by mainstream media for making it. And it is actually fallacious.

If you watch that press conference, he explicitly condemns white supremacists. He does it within 15 seconds or so of the 'fine people' statement. And when he was talking about the fine people, he made it absolutely clear that he was not talking about the white supremacists. He was talking about other people who were out there protesting their statues being taken down. And these are not the people with the tiki torches. These are not members of the KKK.[11]

So, Sam Harris is strong and independent-minded enough to challenge a pillar of his own party's reckless assault on a president he regards as "an existential threat to our democracy." But unlike the 74 million Americans who voted for Trump, and whom Harris dismisses as dishonest, he believes that Trump is such a threat that any lie necessary to take him out of the picture is warranted: "anything that can be made to stick against him should stick because he's an existential threat to our democracy."

Harris made clear the implications of this attitude in connection to the controversy over the Hunter Biden laptop and its effect on the outcome of the 2020 presidential election. As the election approached, the *New York Post* printed an article by Miranda Devine on the contents of the laptop that he had left and then abandoned at a computer repair shop. The owner copied its hard drive and then turned it over to the FBI. The FBI just kept it, remaining silent about its contents for years because of its potential to damage Democrats, and then to defeat Trump in the 2020 election.

When the *New York Post* article appeared shortly before the election, the mainstream media ignored it, and the Big Tech giants who control social media, under pressure from the anti-Trump FBI, blocked the *Post*'s accounts, keeping voters who were outside the conservative bubble in the dark. Their censorship was supported by a public statement signed by the 51 top intelligence officials who perjured themselves, dismissing the contents of the laptop as "Russian disinformation." Only after the election did they admit that the laptop and its contents were authentic.[12]

Trump supporters looked at post-election voter polls to see whether the suppression of the laptop story had affected their votes, and concluded from 17 percent of Biden supporters who said they would have voted differently if the information had been forthcoming, that denying this information had in fact rigged the election in favor of Joe Biden. Recall, Biden "won" the election by 0.027 percent of the vote. That's 44,000 votes out of 159,000,000.[13]

Sam Harris's take on this attack on a presidential election was: well and good; whatever means necessary to defeat Donald Trump. Actually, what he said was worse: "Hunter Biden literally could have had the corpses of children in his basement, I would not have cared," Harris told the Triggernometry podcast. "It's like a firefly to the sun. . . . It doesn't even stack up against Trump University, right? Trump University as a story is worse than anything that can be in Hunter Biden's laptop."[14]

Harris noted how critics called the suppression of the Hunter Biden story "a left-wing conspiracy to deny the presidency to Donald Trump." Harris' response: "Absolutely it was. Absolutely. But I think it was warranted."[15]

Harris is a very smart individual who has devoted much thought to the issues that affect how a democracy exists and thrives. If someone like this is so blinded by hate for a political leader and contempt for his 74 million followers, as to reach the conclusion that suppressing one side of the political conversation is necessary to *save* democracy, consider how such hatred affects ordinary citizens who haven't given a fraction of the thought that Harris has, to what makes a democracy work.

Would not this rationale give such a person—say working in the tech industry—a license to impose themselves on Americans as a censor of thoughts and facts they don't approve? Suppose they were a vote counter during elections, or a postal worker collecting ballots from drop boxes. Wouldn't this give them, and everyone in a position to rig an election—say by stuffing ballot boxes or losing votes—incentive to do so? Isn't this a prescription for the end of democracy rather than its salvation? Isn't it a plausible explanation as to why the fears of those who think the 2020 election was rigged cannot be so easily dismissed? Hasn't this attitude already poisoned the body politic?

If there is an existential threat to American democracy, surely the tsunami of political hate, the condemnation and dismissal of half the population as "white oppressors" and "deplorables" is a prime source of that threat.

SIX

PROGRESSIVE BLINDNESS

Destroy the old, establish the new.

CHINESE CULTURAL REVOLUTION MOTTO

P EOPLE WHO ARE NOT transformational radicals, who do not believe that a perfect world is just over the horizon, are generally bewildered by the failure of the believers to consider the horrifying results of all such projects in the recent past.

In the course of the twentieth century, socialist radicals—Nazis and Communists—left behind a sea of corpses in their efforts to create "new men and new women," or a "master race" that would overcome and leave behind the imperfections of the past. Why are radicals not chastened by these failures, and why do they persist in their arrogant self-image as human gods who can remake the world?

The answer lies in the fundamental nature of radicalism itself. Non-radicals look to the past as a text to instruct them on what human beings are capable of, on what cautions and limits are required to elicit the best in them, and what are necessary to avoid the worst. The American founders were conservatives, who began their constitutional work by studying the record of democracies that had failed.

The genius of the founders was to make the people, not the governors, sovereign, thereby eliminating the threat of tyrannical monarchies. But looking at the history of democracies, and noting how they failed, they also thought to tie the hands of the people themselves with a system of checks and balances that were not democratic. They chose to decide elections in an Electoral College, which could thwart the results of the popular vote. They chose government of the people—but *limited*. They feared popular passions, human deceit, and human greed, and the threat posed by partisan ambitions. Because they feared them so much, they took measures to counter them. They even named their democratic fear: a tyranny of the *majority*.

By way of contrast, a radical disposition begins with the attitude that the past exists not to be learned from, but to be erased in favor of a better future. For radicals, the past is not a guide to the future, but an obstacle on the way to a better world. It is racist, sexist, and classist, a history to be condemned, better forgotten than examined, or examined only as a warning.

The Soviet Union collapsed after seventy years of unsurpassed misery for its citizens. During those years, progressives created and supported one of the most oppressive and bankrupt regimes in all human history. In the wake of this collapse, however, their response was not to analyze the failure and discover why it failed, but to dismiss it wholesale as "not real socialism." Their self-aggrandizing conclusion? "Real socialism has not been tried, and therefore has not failed."

Every revolution begins with a destruction. Every revolutionary is focused on the means to "dismantle" the existing social order, not on devising workable blueprints for the future. Consequently, they are experts at destruction, but criminally incompetent at construction. Their "defund the police" campaign, for example, was a typically ill-thought-out and instantly disastrous remedy for urban violence. It was based not on a serious assessment of human nature and the actual problems it poses but on an ideological hatred of law enforcement. Cops, in their view, were an "occupying army" that served the ruling class—*pigs* who had to be confronted and vanquished before "social justice" could be created.

Therefore, they didn't pause to wonder what the consequences of eliminating the police might be. Their inability to assess the impact on human behavior of what they were demanding led to an explosion of violent crime and thousands of defenseless victims.

There is, however, one radical expertise, which comes from centuries of working to dismantle existing social orders. This expertise lies in dissembling about their actual agendas, infiltrating institutions, and undermining the authority of society's foundational contracts. "The Constitution is actually trash," Harvard Law School graduate, former Debevoise & Plimpton lawyer, and MSNBC commentator Elie Mystal sums up their nihilistic view. Mystal is, not incidentally, the "justice correspondent" for *The Nation*, a magazine that has supported every Communist dictatorship and enemy of the United States since World War II.

Mystal's rationale for dismissing the Constitution, which is the social contract under which the United States became the most prosperous, free, and inclusive nation in the world, is that it was written by white men: "We act like this thing was kind of etched in stone by the finger of God, when actually it was hotly contested and debated, scrawled out over a couple of weeks in the summer in Philadelphia in 1787, with a bunch of rich, white politicians making deals with each other."[16] What is trash is racist non-thinking like this, which is the dominant point of view in our once-premier institutions of "higher learning."

Radicals propose to replace the Constitution's "trash" with a regime of "social justice." Half a century ago, Friedrich Hayek explained why the very concept of "social justice" was meaningless.[17] Society is not an entity that can distribute justice, or anything for that matter. There is no entity "society"; there are only individuals and the factions they form to accumulate power.

When a progressive administration distributes trillions of dollars to advance "social justice," what is actually transpiring is quite different. The main beneficiaries of the largesse will inevitably be the ruling party's donors and voters. In a democracy, votes are the source of power. Whatever agenda a political faction seeks to advance can only be implemented if the faction accumulates more power. Redistributing taxpayer monies to donors and supporters is therefore an irresistible temptation if one is serious about one's goals. Redistributing wealth to oneself serves the necessary quest for power but is hardly *just*.

Between 1965 and 2016, the American government poured some $27.8 trillion of taxpayer funds into welfare programs designed to eliminate poverty.[18] We see the results all around us: Every major inner city in America is 100 percent controlled by progressives in the Democrat Party and has been for 50 to 100 years. Therefore, every "injustice" in America's inner cities—off-the-charts crime and unemployment rates, out-of-wedlock births, massive school dropouts, soul-crushing poverty—is 100 percent the result of the monopoly rule of the inner cities by progressives and Democrats.

Nearly thirty *trillion* dollars invested in the "War on Poverty" over more than half a century have failed to reduce poverty rates one iota. If black Americans are suffering, marginalized, and under-served, Democrats are responsible, despite their "social justice" sweet talk.

Equally destructive is the fact that all attempts by government to redistribute wealth—which is the heart of the social justice mission—necessarily entail treating citizens *un*equally. This is because people are born unequal in intelligence, beauty, physical ability, talent, dedication, and discipline—all factors contributing to unequal incomes. To achieve a more "just" distribution, then, it is necessary for the government to treat its citizens *un*equally, privileging some above others—in other words, to create new injustices. Do we want the government to systematically treat people unequally, like all hierarchical societies? Is it beneficial to people to put money in their hands that they haven't earned? The permanent underclass that Democrats have created in America's inner cities would argue a resounding *no*.

AN OUTLAW MENTALITY

Everyone in Washington understands the basic causes of inflation. If the government prints more money than it can back up with real assets like gold, it devalues the currency and makes everything cost more. If the government declares war on fossil fuels, shuts down pipelines, closes vast oil fields like ANWR, and doesn't approve drilling licenses generally, those actions cause the price of everything to go up, because virtually everything requires energy to produce. If the government prints and distributes vast amounts of money, inducing individuals not to work, employers will raise wages to entice them to work, and that, too, will cause prices to go up.[19] Everyone, but especially those on the lower rungs of the economic ladder, will suffer. It's not rocket science.

Despite understanding these consequences, the Biden progressives have instituted all of these inflationary measures, breaking all spending records while taking no responsibility for their effects and the suffering they cause. They did this to advance their progressive agenda, which has not changed its fundamental premises since 1848, when Marx published what is, and has always been, the basic blueprint for progressive schemes.

The Biden reactionaries deny their responsibility for the costly and dangerous inflation their policies have created in the way they normally cover up their assaults on the public: with two obvious lies. First by claiming the inflation was "transitory,"[20] and then by blaming it on the Russians—calling it "Putin's price hike."[21] They even passed an "Inflation Reduction" bill, which every non-partisan agency says will not reduce inflation, but which does allocate billions for their donors and supporters in the name of "climate change."

The brazen character of these lies, and the fact that Biden repeats them in the face of devastating refutations, reflects the fact that the Democrats know full well what they are doing. They are building their army and financing their transformational agendas with public debt even though it means stoking the fires of a volatile inflation that is causing profound hardship to the very constituencies they pretend to care about.

Runaway inflation is not just damaging to the working and middle classes. It has the power to destroy entire societies. Money is a social glue. It provides incentives to work and to be law-abiding. It is a bargaining chip that can deflect and avoid social violence. It is an incentive to work and gain independence, which is vital to human well-being. When the value of money is destroyed, an indispensable social bond is destroyed as well. That is what happened to the Weimar Republic in the 1920s and led to the election of Adolf Hitler in 1933.

What, then, could the Democrats be thinking in pouring fuel on the fires of inflation? The Biden Democrats, who have dumped trillions of dollars on an already heated economy, look on the United States Treasury as a bank that can be robbed in the interests of buying votes, accumulating power, and ushering in their new world.

Are electric cars and renewable energies expensive? Provide subsidies. Print more money. Progressives consider the bulk of tax receipts to be ill-gotten gains of the rich, which it is their mission to redistribute to their friends. They feel further licensed to empty the nation's bank because of the nobility of their mission, which is to "save the planet." In their eyes, the money represents the fruits of exploitation made possible by a "white supremacist" capitalist system. In such a system, money is not earned but is extracted by socially sanctioned power. It is a system that they are bound not to respect.

The money progressives rob from the nation's bank will be redistributed according to the dictates of social justice—a yardstick based on their political ambitions and social whims. In the name of social justice, for example, the Biden regime has allocated $7.5 billion to put a black female astronaut on the moon *because* she is black and female.[22] This is a preposterous virtue signal that only those who are drunk with the idea that they are "on the right side of history" can take seriously. Worse, it violates the very spirit of America's color- and gender-blind

Constitution. But progressives, who have no respect for the Constitution, needn't be bothered by that.

Unfortunately, Republicans, and conservatives generally, are too polite to embarrass their political opponents by pointing out the criminal nature of their agendas and their *modus operandi.* The harshest words Republicans will use to describe the Democrats' campaign to free hundreds of thousands of violent criminals, defund the police, and stimulate a national crime wave is that they are "soft on crime."

Democrats—*progressives*—are not *soft* on crime, they are *pro-crime.*[23] They regard crime as a primitive form of social justice. Mobs of mainly black predators looting department stores in broad daylight is to them reparations—a socialist redistribution of income that provides equity to a group allegedly—but never specifically—oppressed.[24]

Sixty years ago, the Communist historian Eric Hobsbawm wrote a book, widely praised on the left, called *Primitive Rebels.* It was about criminal gangs in ninteenth-century Sicily, whom he saw as Marxists *avant la lettre.* In other words, their criminality would have been seen as social justice if they had advanced their malignant agendas in the language of progressives like himself.

Hobsbawm, by the way, was showered with academic honors in America, notwithstanding his lifelong service to Stalin's Russia and his admission that he had no regrets about the tens of millions of victims his comrades had slaughtered on their way to the new world. To Hobsbawm the promise of a socialist paradise was so great that it was worth the risk that another 40 million innocents might be slaughtered to achieve it the next time.

SOCIALISM IS THEFT

Progressivism is ultimately a criminal mentality. By progressivism, I mean every political philosophy that regards itself as revolutionary, or transformative—describes itself as socialist, communist, fascist, or jihadist—and believes that "the moral arc of the universe bends towards justice." The belief that the world is marching towards justice, and that to be a progressive means one is "on the right side of history," is a delusion that will justify any and every atrocity, and already has.

This is why today's progressives are advancing the same genocidal agendas that the Western nations defeated in World War II and the Cold War. The "Progressive Caucus"[25] in Congress, and its racist leaders—Pramila Jayapal, Rashida Tlaib, Ilhan Omar, AOC, and Ayanna Pressley—are in full-throated support of the 75-year genocidal campaign against the Jews, conducted by the terrorist dictatorships in Gaza and the West Bank.[26]

On a less apocalyptic level, the criminal nature of the progressive outlook should be obvious to anyone who takes the time to look at its domestic legislative agenda. Virtually every progressive proposal, from the moratorium on rent payments to canceling student debts to handing out other people's money to their favored constituents for doing nothing, is an eloquent expression of the fact that socialism is theft.

Student loans guaranteed by the federal government were a progressive legislative achievement. They led directly to a rampant inflation of student fees as university administrators raised tuition rates because they could.[27] The student loan "victims" championed by progressives weren't forced to take loans, nor did anyone twist their arms to spend the money on frivolous courses in woke agendas, which would likely not lead to jobs allowing them to repay their debts. But now that the student loan program as designed by them is a burden on those who took advantage of it, the progressive solution is to make taxpayers—including students who did pay their debts— foot the bill for those who couldn't be bothered to.[28] Theft.

THE UNBEARABLE LIGHTNESS OF BERNIE

What progressives can never quite fathom, what they adamantly deny, is that people are naturally *un*equal. The *Declaration*'s dedication to equality is to equality in the eyes of God, and therefore before the law, whose basic rights are the gifts of God and therefore "unalienable." On the other hand, inequality to progressives is not a reflection of human nature, but the result of exploitation, oppression, sexism, and racism by white males.

Bernie Sanders is the founder of the Progressive Caucus and the most popular figure in the Democrat Party. He is also the Chairman of the Senate Budget Committee and therefore a key player in determining how Washington decides to spend taxpayers' dollars. Bernie is also a lifetime fan of Communist regimes and an apologist for their totalitarian practices—and atrocities. He supported Iran's Islamofascist regime in 1979 when it made hostages of 52 American diplomats and embassy workers, held them for 444 days, and chanted, "Death to America" and "Death to Israel"—repeating the threats through time.[29]

As an American politician for more than five decades, Bernie's chief passion has been hatred of the wealthy, and of the economic system that makes wealth possible. He pursues this passion without a scintilla of self-awareness, ignoring the fact that he, himself, is worth $3 million, even though he has never held a significant private-sector job.[30]

This personal wealth allows him to own three houses, while the average person is lucky to own one. While presenting himself as a champion of the working classes, and an opponent of million-dollar incomes, he has no apparent intention of redistributing his own wealth to less-fortunate individuals who may need it more than he does.

Without the slightest sense of irony, Bernie boasts that his first priority as a politician is to make socialist theft the law of the land, using the power of the state to force the most successful people to fork over their earnings and allow him as budget chairman to spend them. Here is how his 2020 presidential campaign spokesman embellished this social injustice: "The record shows that from the very beginning, Bernie anticipated and worked to combat the rise of a billionaire ruling class and the exploding power of Wall Street and multinational corporations."[31]

Specifically, Bernie hoped to accomplish this transfer by passing a law that would make it illegal for anyone to accumulate more wealth than he or she could spend in a lifetime. Under Bernie's law, any income above $1 million per year would be taxed at a rate of 100 percent. "Nobody should earn more than a million dollars," Bernie explained in 1974, before he became a multi-millionaire himself, and shifted his attention to billionaires.[32]

In keeping with his determination to lead a campaign against wealth, whether earned or not, Bernie's Twitter feed is monotonously filled with jeremiads about how bad, unfair, and obscene it is for CEOs of large corporations to make more money than their workers. The following is a typical snark: "CEOs at large corporations are paid 350x more than what their average worker makes. Is that the kind of economic reality we should accept? I don't think so."[33]

At this point, one might be prompted to ask: What educational or job experience can Bernie claim that would even suggest he had the credentials to draw such a society-changing conclusion affecting the lives of three hundred million Americans? The answer is *none*.

In 1964, Bernie graduated with a bachelor's degree in political science from the University of Chicago. While at UC, Sanders joined the Young People's Socialist League, an ideological perspective he took with him when he went to work as an organizer for the Student Nonviolent Coordinating Committee.[34] This radical component of the civil rights movement was led by Stokely Carmichael, a rabid anti-Semite, notorious for his claim that "the only good Zionist is a dead Zionist." Carmichael was also a black racist who invented the slogan "Black Power" to challenge Martin Luther King's leadership of what was then an inter-racial movement dedicated to non-violence and inter-racial peace. Carmichael then expelled all the whites in his organization, a large number of whom were Jews.[35]

Nominally, Bernie is a Jew. But all of Bernie's Jewish connections, including the kibbutz he spent time on in Israel, were organizations run by anti-Israel, anti-American, pro-Arab Marxists, just as his stateside political bases were anti-American, pro-Castro, and pro-Soviet. Typical was his membership in the Jewish Zionist group Hashomer Hatzair, whose founder, Ya'akov Hazan, described the USSR as a second homeland

and in 1953 put on sack cloth and ashes because of what he described as "the terrible tragedy that has befallen the nations of the Soviet Union, the world proletariat, and all of progressive mankind, upon the death of the great leader and extolled commander, Josef Vissarionovich Stalin."[36]

Before turning to a full-time political career, Bernie participated in a Quaker project at a California psychiatric hospital and worked briefly as an organizer for the left-wing United Packinghouse Workers Union. He then moved to Vermont—a radical Mecca—where he worked variously as a carpenter, filmmaker, writer, and researcher.[37]

This survey of Bernie's early absorption in an ideological war that was anti-capitalist, anti-American, and anti-business should make obvious why his mature views are so ignorant of the basic workings of the economic system that has made him a multi-millionaire via funds donated to his campaigns to change the world. He remains stubbornly oblivious to the fact that this same economic system has created the greatest prosperity and freedom for those who live under it in the history of mankind.

Let's put the question bluntly then: Would reducing the pay of a corporate CEO to what one of his average workers makes benefit anyone who is connected to the corporation or dependent on its earnings? The only way the answer could be *yes* would be if anyone can run a corporation. Unfortunately (and obviously), this is not the case.

Steve Jobs co-founded Apple and ran it for years as a thriving company until he was forced out during a power struggle with its board. John Sculley, who replaced him, was an accomplished corporate executive who had run PepsiCo. But the minute Sculley was running Apple without Jobs, its earnings and stock price began to tank until it teetered on the edge of bankruptcy.

In practice, this meant that all its average workers were in imminent danger of having their wages reduced or being laid off. Hundreds of thousands of ordinary people who owned stock in Apple had already lost significant portions of their investments. Bernie's socialist delusions, if put into practice, would punish not only CEOs but all the average workers dependent on their judgments and skills to make the companies that provided their income successful.

While he was exiled from Apple, the talented Jobs founded two new hugely successful corporations: the animated filmmaker Pixar and the computer company NeXT. In 1996, Apple bought NeXT for $427 million, bringing Jobs back to the company, whose board quickly made him interim chief executive. Immediately, Apple's stock began to rise, and under Jobs's restored leadership, Apple eventually became the largest corporation in the world.

Business genius commands a high price because everyone whose prosperity depends on a company's success benefits when the company is successful. The economic reality of which Bernie is so ignorant is this: business genius, like all genius, is not fungible; people are not equal, and in a just world their rewards will be commensurate with their contributions to others, even if that makes them 350x richer than the average worker they employ.

Elon Musk is worth $273 billion, which makes him the richest person in the world. His achievements show that he may also be the smartest—certainly among the smartest. He graduated from the University of Pennsylvania in 1994 at the age of 23, having majored in business and physics. The following year, he and his brother cofounded a company, funded by angel investors, called Zip2. At the time, Musk could not afford an apartment and instead rented an office, slept on its couch, showered at the YMCA, and worked round the clock, seven days a week, programming.

In 1999, Musk sold Zip2 for $307 million. Musk's share was $22 million. He was 28 years old. That same year, Musk co-founded X.com, an online financial services and e-mail payment company. The following year, X.com merged with the online bank Confinity, which became PayPal. In 2002, PayPal was acquired by eBay for $1.5 billion in stock, of which Musk, the largest shareholder, received $175.8 million.

The preceding year, Musk had become involved with the nonprofit Mars Society. He was inspired by their plans to place a growth chamber for plants on Mars and discussed funding the project himself. In October 2001, Musk traveled to Moscow to buy refurbished intercontinental ballistic missiles (ICBMs) that could send the greenhouse payloads into space. The Russians were uncooperative, and the mission failed, but the following year Musk invested $100 million of his own money to found SpaceX, as a company that could build affordable rockets. Twenty-two years later, after several successful flights in space, it is safe to say that without Musk's SpaceX investments, the United States would still not have a space program.

In 2004, Musk invested $6.5 million in Tesla, Inc., a fledgling electric car company, and became its largest shareholder, joining its board as chairman. In 2008, Tesla built an electric sports car, the Roadster. With sales of about 2,500 vehicles, it was the first serial production all-electric car to use lithium-ion battery cells. A mass-market sedan, the Model 3 was released in 2017. Three years later, it had become the world's best-selling electric car, with more than 500,000 units delivered. It has been estimated that Musk advanced the production and use of electric vehicles by 20 years. In October 2021, Tesla reached a market capitalization of $1 trillion, only the sixth company to do so in U.S. history.

These are only some of this remarkable man's achievements. It would not do to omit the fact that during the Russian invasion of Ukraine, Moscow's cyber attacks took out the Ukrainian Internet, isolating the Ukrainian defenders from each other. Musk immediately restored the Ukrainian Internet, providing a vital tool for Ukraine's defenses.

Elon Musk's career shows how utterly worthless progressive ideas are about the economy, about human motivations, about economic inequality, and about the dread profit motive. Obviously, Musk's plans to grow plants on Mars, which led to the creation of SpaceX, or to create electric cars, were not motivated by greed or monetary gain. If you are a billionaire, and $100 million is but a tenth of your portfolio account, personal money is virtually meaningless. The other $900 million will produce $50 million a year if invested modestly. Musk himself has said that physical things mean nothing to him, and it is easy to see why this could be so.[38]

The irony is that Musk had motivations similar to those of leftist missionaries wanting to change the world and make it a better place. But unlike leftists, who think that destroying the system that made a Musk possible would pave the way to a glorious future, Musk took advantage of the amazing economic system—capitalism—that empowers individuals like himself and makes monumental schemes like taming outer space feasible.

The left's sinister stupidity is summed up in its demands to replace the market system with "production for people not profit." This slogan merely demonstrates the mind-numbing ignorance of leftist missionaries. Criminal money-making schemes aside, how is it possible to make profits if one doesn't serve people?

Profit is a measure of efficiency; it is produced by increasing revenues and lowering costs. Profit is an *incentive* to meet people's needs and satisfy their desires. Why was Amazon the greatest beneficiary of the COVID-19 pandemic? Because its leaders found the most efficient and satisfying way to allow people to shop from their own homes during a pandemic. Are there dishonest merchants who will try to pass off inferior goods to customers to create unjustifiable profits? Yes. But that is a failing of human nature—of ethics, not profits. Moreover, in a competitive system, if you try to multiply profits by cheating customers, eventually you will fail.

These observations lead us back to a consideration of the most destructive blind spot of the progressive outlook: the refusal to recognize the fundamental inequality of human beings and their capabilities. This refusal is manifest in their inability to appreciate the unique and socially invaluable genius of entrepreneurs like Steve Jobs and Elon Musk, and instead respond to them with a destructive hatred born of envy and resentment, which are the key passions of the progressive mind. It also leads directly to an inability to appreciate the insurmountable obstacles to their utopian schemes.

To belabor the point, there are 60,000 songs *a day* submitted to the Internet music publisher Spotify by aspiring entertainment stars. There are millions, then, of such individuals. But there are only a couple of thousand people who are talented enough to fill Madison Square Garden or a sports stadium and earn millions of dollars in a single night. Superstars like Bob Dylan and Eric Clapton, who can fill such venues are personally worth in excess of $400 million each.[39] Did they earn that money? Is their music worth their earnings? Millions of customers to whom their music has brought solace and pleasure say it is. Even if they make 350 times what the average worker in their organizations make.

Steph Curry is the greatest shooter in the history of basketball. He makes $46 million a year from his salary as a Golden State Warrior. There are players on the Warriors' roster who make only $200,000 or roughly 230 times less.[40] There are members of the Warriors' organization who earn less than that—maybe 350 times less.

Curry is well rewarded because he is a "franchise player." His talent is so great, and the show he puts on such a fan draw, that his team fills the arena every night over the course of an eighty-plus-game season and earns the Warrior organization billions of dollars. Every dollar that Bernie Sanders wants to take from Steph Curry in the name of social justice is a dollar stolen from a man who earned it, and from all the average workers and stakeholders in his organization who benefit from his talents. Socialism is theft.

Bernie Sanders's progressive myopia puts me in mind of a joke I was told as a child. A small individual confronts a very large one with this challenge: "If I were as big as you, I would be heavyweight champion of the world." "Oh, yeah?" comes the reply, "Why aren't you lightweight champion?"

Bernie Sanders's hate-filled outrage at the inequality of reward between a CEO and the average worker in his company stems from an obtuse denial of the inequality of intelligence, skills, and judgment distributed among human beings—a diversity that is characteristic of all humanity. It is the inequality of capabilities that translates into an inequality of rewards. The cry for an impossible dream of social justice—a world of equals—is a crime against humanity and its diversity. Its motivations are envy, resentment, and hate. It is social *injustice* personified, an attempt to steal the unequal rewards and powers that accrue to individuals who have earned them, and who possess the talents—if they don't abuse them—to make life for all of us better.

THE HIERARCHY OF OPPRESSION

Perhaps the most common conservative reaction to progressive ideas about the present state of the society they seek to dismantle and transform is one of bewilderment. *They're from a different planet; they inhabit an alternate universe; they're insane.* Even moderates employ these phrases to express their inability to understand the progressive mentality. And this is so, even in regard to problems like crime that traditionally have provided common ground for partisan factions. Thus, the 1994 Crime Bill—also known as the Clinton Crime Bill and the Biden Crime Bill for its sponsors—was passed by an overwhelming bipartisan majority in Congress.[41]

Yet today it is anathema to progressives, whose ideology has shifted and who now see violent criminals as victims of an unjust criminal justice system, and theft as a form of reparations. Extreme reversals like this have prompted liberal dissenters like Joe Manchin, Bill Maher, and former congressman Harold Ford to express support for conservative concerns that progressives are "out of touch with reality" and that their views "lack common sense."[42] The criminal justice system may need reform, but mass releases of violent criminals is hardly the reform it needs.

The obvious explanation for progressive failure to connect with a reality that even moderates readily see, is that progressives don't actually *see* reality. Ideological blinders block its complexities and frustrate their ability to appreciate the obvious. As Hamlet admonished his courtier friend: "There are more things in heaven and earth, Horatio, than are dreamt of in your philosophy."

An ideology is like a prism in which some planes simply don't appear or are so distorted they might as well not. The progressive prism refracts all social issues into three categories of race, gender, and class. Complexities like cultural differences among groups, or individual psychologies and behaviors, are not part of the progressive spectrum. Consequently, for progressives they don't exist, or, if they do, don't matter and are readily dismissed.

The result of these optic deficiencies are crackpot pronouncements that bewilder the politically incorrect. Certainly, the most important (and perhaps the most bizarre) of these pronouncements is the progressive claim that, "America is a white supremacist society, which marginalizes and underserves people of color." This is the kind of statement the Biden White House makes when explaining its "equity" policies, which are designed to correct the injustice.[43]

But if this description is accurate, how does one explain the presence of two million or more people—mainly "of color"—annually massing at America's southern border, and risking their lives to get into a country, which is said to oppress them?[44] Why would an estimated two million "people of color" decide to trek a thousand miles through jungles and other natural perils this year alone to break into a white supremacist country that will marginalize, underserve, and oppress them?

The spectrum of progressive ideology is always seen by those who are drunk on it as a "hierarchy of oppression." This so-called hierarchy has been turned into an elaborate and lucrative enterprise, generating mountains of hot air in the academy, where it is called the "theory of intersectionality." This ludicrous exercise in intellectual thumb-sucking assigns levels of so-called oppression to individuals who are alleged to have multiple "oppressed" identities, which rank them in a hierarchy of victimhood. Thus, black lesbian females are said to be more oppressed than heterosexual black males.

But are they? Are black lesbian females really powerless in twenty-first century America? At the bottom of the totem pole? Victims of multiple oppressions that render them powerless? All the founding organizers of Black Lives Matter, who were able to recruit an estimated 40 million supporters in the summer of 2020, and to orchestrate violent attacks on nearly 220 cities,[45] and to collect nearly $100 million in donations from America's richest corporations and celebrities,[46] and were officially endorsed by the president of the United States and the Democrat Party[47]—*all* the creators and leaders of Black Lives Matter able to accomplish these feats are black lesbians—and proud of it.[48] Victims indeed. More accurately: victimizers.

The federal government has spent tens of millions of tax-payers' dollars on fatuous intersectionality projects without managing to provide a reasonable explanation of what constitutes "oppression" in a free society or how individuals can be trapped at various levels of a "hierarchy" in a nation where everyone is guaranteed equal rights by law.

However vacuous, the term "oppression" still has a powerful emotional charge, which is why radicals who are determined to demonize Americans and dismantle our society find it so useful as a weapon. "Oppression" is an ancient term with a distinctive etymology that provides its emotional power. Twenty-five hundred years ago, the Jews were oppressed as slaves in Egypt. The story of their oppression and exodus to freedom has been memorialized and celebrated in the foundational literature of Western civilization.

The noun "oppression" derives its power from these antecedents. When we say the heat is "oppressive," it has a specific meaning: it's time to get out of the sun. No group in America—except children of abusive parents and the victims of sex traffickers, slavers, and misogynistic criminals—is oppressed. No racial, gender, or economic group is oppressed. If they are, where is the exodus?

Are black Americans marginalized? Blacks have been the center of the nation's attention since the civil rights movement of the 1950s. Although comprising only 13 percent of the population, they have been able to assert themselves as an unrivalled force in the nation's media, music, and entertainment cultures. Through their dominant roles in sports, black athletes have provided icons and role models for generations of America's youth—black and white. They are the chief executives in most of America's major cities. They hold—or have held—the highest offices in the land. How marginal is that?

Are black Americans underserved? In fact, they have been the focus of federal support and privileges amounting to trillions of dollars—more than any other ethnic or racial group. From the point of view of opportunities and benefactions offered on the basis of skin color, there is no greater "skin privilege" than being black.

Intersectional hierarchies with an oppressor caste of white males at the top are a progressive illusion. There is no such closed social hierarchy possible in America. The alleged oppressor caste—white males—are only about a third of the population. The putative victims of their oppression not only outnumber them 2:1, they are endowed with the same voting powers and civil rights. So how are white males able to control and oppress this majority?

Women preside over courts, run major law enforcement agencies, occupy the vice presidency, sit on the Supreme Court, are the most powerful members of the House of Representatives, have chaired both political parties, are members of the military brass, are police chiefs and prosecutors and attorneys general, and the chief executives of major American cities. If there hasn't been a female president yet, whose fault is that? Clearly not white males.

Is there a glass ceiling for women? The phrase itself is a giveaway that there is not. If the ceiling is invisible, it's because it doesn't exist. The gender-wage gap is a long-disproven fiction.[49] Wage discrimination against women was outlawed as a practice nearly 60 years ago by the Equal Pay for Equal Work Act of 1963—passed by a Congress almost exclusively male.

If such a gap existed, and wasn't outlawed, the remedy would be to do what the Jews and the Irish did when prejudice made them social pariahs. They built their own institutions.

Do women have the resources to create their own economies? Indeed, they do. In America, women's wealth amounts to $11 trillion, more than enough to build equal pay for equal work institutions if the law didn't already require it.[50]

What is true for glass ceilings is also true for concepts like "unconscious racism," "implicit racism," and "unintentional racism," all weasel words deployed to justify the aggressive anti-white racism of the diversity industry, and fight imaginary foes. If the racism is unconscious and unintentional, then it is in the eye of the beholder. It doesn't exist, and if it did, it would be easily corrected by a wagging finger.

"Triggering" moments are not oppressions of groups trapped in a rigid hierarchy from which they cannot escape. If too many black Americans are poor, the source of their poverty is themselves and the choices they make. In fact, only 20 percent of black Americans are poor.[51] Better if it were fewer, but that figure poses the question: If 80 percent of blacks are not poor, how can racism be the explanation for the failure of 20 percent to avail themselves of the advantages that are open to the other 80 percent? Especially when there are millions of people here illegally, who don't speak the language, and still manage to earn a decent living.

Among the more obvious holes in the progressive world view is the fact that there is no place for history, except as a locus of bad practices that can be manipulated to indict the present. The facts that American slaves were first enslaved by black Africans who sold them at auctions in Africa, and that white

Americans died in the hundreds of thousands to free blacks and also inspired a global movement for equal rights for all, is missing from progressive narratives or dismissed out of hand.

The progressive outlook has no place for the crucial roles that psychology, family structure, or criminal behavior play in the destinies not only of individuals but of groups. The progressive outlook also has no room for the idea that attitudes can change, and not only under threat. Above all, it has no appreciation for the long-term benefits of a society, like America's, which fosters upward mobility and was dedicated in its founding in a hierarchical world to provide equal rights for all.

The fight against a master race in World War II had a profound but little-appreciated effect on white attitudes—one that triggered the greatest social revolution in human history. This revolution was aided by the mass migration of blacks from the rural South, which had high rates of poverty for all races, to the industrial North.[52]

Between 1940 and 1950, the earnings of the average black male increased 75 percent, which was about twice the rate at which white incomes grew.[53] This was *before* the civil rights movement, the Civil Rights Act of 1964 and the Great Society welfare programs that, in any case, failed to reduce poverty at all. Between 1940 and 1960, black incomes for males and females more than doubled.[54] By 1971, oppressed, marginalized, and underserved black couples with two working spouses were earning 5 percent more than white couples of the same description in every part of the United States except the South.[55]

Inflation-adjusted *per capita* black income in 1973 was more than 125 percent higher than twenty-five years earlier.[56] Since 1981, black families with two college-educated, working spouses have earned slightly more than white families of the same description in every age group and in every region of the country.[57]

Why have 20 percent of the black population failed to climb out of poverty, while 80 percent have succeeded? Here is one well-known statistic, dismissed by progressives, that helps to explain. In 2019, the poverty rate in traditional two-parent families of all races was 4 percent, compared with 22.2 percent in families headed by a female with no adult male present.[58]

Why are 70 percent of black families in inner cities single-parent, female-headed households?[59] Because 60 years ago progressives devised a welfare system that disqualifies families with a father in the home from receiving welfare benefits. Progressive ideology—not race—is the oppressor of black poor people in America.

The statistics show that income equality is within the power of blacks to achieve by themselves. Whites are richer not because they oppress blacks but because whites are more successful at forming traditional nuclear families and completing a college education. The educational system is public and largely free, especially to government-privileged minorities.

Black failure is concentrated in urban centers where progressives administer school systems that are perfectly comfortable with 40 percent dropout rates, and 40 percent functional illiteracy rates among those who do manage to graduate. The failure to educate inner-city minority children is a social atrocity for which a hundred years of progressive rule is responsible, with no end in sight.

Donald Trump was a threat to this unconscionable state of affairs. Trump launched his 2016 presidential campaign by proposing a voucher program to liberate inner-city minority families from a permanently failed school system run for the benefit of the progressive teachers' unions and the Democrat Party. In a speech in Michigan, he said: "No group in America has been more harmed by [Democrat] policies than African Americans. No group. No group. If [the Democrats'] goal was to inflict pain on the African American community, [they] could not have done a better job. It's a disgrace."[60]

Then Trump posed this challenge: "Tonight, I'm asking for the vote of every African American citizen in this country who wants to see a better future. Look how much African American communities have suffered under Democratic control. To those I say the following: What do you have to lose by trying something new, like Trump? You're living in poverty. Your schools are no good. You have no jobs. Fifty-eight percent of your youth is unemployed. What the hell do you have to lose?"[61]

The Democrats' response to this challenge was to call Trump a "racist," a "white nationalist," "mentally unstable," "morally disreputable," and "a would-be dictator." When the *Detroit News* asked a local black pastor, "What do you have to lose?" the pastor said, "We have *everything* to lose by voting for him. This man is a bigot."[62] Outside of Democrat slanders, there is no evidence whatsoever that Donald Trump is a bigot. Quite the opposite.

The chief support for the unconscionable injustices suffered by inner-city minorities is the unending stream of anti-white racism that pours out of the Biden White House, the Democrat Party, Black Lives Matter, the leftwing media, the corporate culture, universities, philanthropic institutions, the diversity industry, and the K–12 teacher unions. The sinister message to black Americans from all of these race-infected institutions is: *You don't control your destiny, racist whites do. Republicans are white supremacists. Put your trust in us.*

These lies have planted the seeds of violent hatred, triggering a national crime wave. The chief effect of anti-white racism is to cancel conservative critiques of the injustices in the communities Democrats control. The racist indictment of whites also inculcates a sense of powerlessness that encourages segments of the black community to put their faith in corrupt leaders who, over the years, have pocketed billions of taxpayers' dollars originally earmarked for those left behind. Trump is a threat because he has won support from greater percentages of the black community than any Republican before him.

Anti-white racism insulates progressive exploiters of the poor from the scrutiny necessary to achieve the institutional changes needed to end their oppression of the inner-city poor. What are specifically needed is school reform, family support, and the toughening and enforcement of anti-drug laws.

There is no hierarchy of oppression in America's constitutional order. But there *are* such hierarchies in the socialist societies admired by progressives: Cuba, China, Venezuela, Nicaragua, and Russia. The social hierarchy in these countries is determined by the hierarchy in the ruling party that bills itself as the savior of the people, which is precisely how progressives see themselves. This produces a contrasting attitude toward conservatives who resist them, summed up by Speaker Pelosi: they are "enemies of the state."[63]

DEFENSE OF THE REPUBLIC

T HE PRESENT BATTLE FOR America's soul will take generations to resolve. It is a battle that pits America's defenders—believers in ordered liberty—against believers in the unlimited power and authority of the state. In the conflicts that ensue, the two institutions that will lead the defense of America's constitutional order are the American family, and members—or respecters—of Judeo-Christian religions.

Already the revolt against the progressive assault in the schools is being led by parents who are outraged by the efforts of teachers' unions to come between them and their children, to enlist the defenseless, innocent young, in racist attacks on their country and its freedoms, and to inflict on them life-altering drugs and ungrounded attitudes about "gender fluidity" and transgenderism, as part of their plan to "change the world."

The family, for better or worse, is the shaper of values and the first defender of individual freedoms against the intrusions of the state. The health of society rises and falls with the health and strength of the family and its bonds. A decent society will be one that defends families against the intrusion of outside forces, ideological and governmental, which seek to capture its children to serve their destructive agendas.

The second institutional pillar of the nation's defense is religion—specifically, the principles embraced and the

communities formed by members of Judeo-Christian religions. One doesn't have to be a believer in divine origins, or
trust in a divine destiny, to appreciate the fact that America's
constitutional order was the creation of believing Christians,
whose vision was shaped by the doctrines of the Protestant
Reformation.

American freedoms and America's revolutionary ideal of
equality can all be traced to the Christian values associated
with Martin Luther and his disciples. Thomas Jefferson did not
believe in the divinity of Christ, but he did rely on his biblical
faith and what it taught him about human nature and human
behavior, which led him to champion these values.

Every freedom enjoyed by Americans is a gift of the faith
that was bestowed upon them, not by a government of men,
but by a divinity. Therefore, there is no human authority that
can take them away. *They are unalienable.*

Radicals hate religious communities because they are based
on allegiance to a higher power and stronger moral authority
than the political state. They are the defenders of the private
sphere, of the freedom of conscience and its expression, which
is the basis of all the freedoms we have.

The hour is late, and the forces of darkness are upon us.
To save our freedoms, Americans must renew their faith in
their country, relearn its history, re-acquaint themselves with
the wisdom of the founders, and reject the siren songs of the
envious, the resentful, and the haters of human diversity who
have malice in their hearts.

NOTES

Chapter One

1. https://www.wsj.com/articles/100-years-of-communismand-100 -million-dead-1510011810.

2. https://www.marxists.org/archive/trotsky/1938/morals/morals.htm.

3. I was provided this historical reference by Professor Jay Bergman, author of *The French Revolutionary Tradition in Russian and Soviet Politics, Political Thought, and Culture*, 2019.

4. https://www.cubacenter.org/archives/2021/6/30/cubabrief-sixty -years-ago-today-castro-declared-to-artists-and-intellectuals -within-the-revolution-everything-outside-of-it-nothing-and -the-dictatorship-continues-to-jail-free-thinkers-today.

5. https://www.dailymail.co.uk/tvshowbiz/article-2678654/Jane -Fondas-son-Troy-Garity-wears-communist-themed-T-shirt -grabs-coffee-Hollywood.html.

6. https://www.fox13now.com/2014/11/20/republicans-hammer -legal-case-against-obama-on-immigration; https://townhall .com/tipsheet/katiepavlich/2014/11/19/jon-karl-does-obama -think-hes-emperor-of-the-united-states-n1920606.

7. https://www.cnn.com/2014/11/20/politics/republican-response -obama-immigration-speech/index.html.

8. https://obamawhitehouse.archives.gov/realitycheck/the-press -office/2011/03/28/remarks-president-univision-town-hall.

9. https://www.texastribune.org/2011/07/25/obama-on -immigration-reform-blame-republicans/.

10. https://townhall.com/tipsheet/katiepavlich/2014/11/19/jon-karl -does-obama-think-hes-emperor-of-the-united-states-n1920606.

11. Stanley Kurtz: *Radical-in-Chief,* 2010 and David Horowitz, *Barack Obama's Rules for Revolution,* 2009.

12. https://www.uscis.gov/humanitarian/consideration-of-deferred -action-for-childhood-arrivals-daca.

13. https://www.uscis.gov/archive/2014-executive-actions-on -immigration

14. https://www.nbcchicago.com/news/local/black-lives-matter -holds-rally-supporting-individuals-arrested-in-chicago-looting -monday/2320365/.

15. https://thehill.com/blogs/blog-briefing-room/news/416189-most -dems-view-republicans-racist-and-sexist-poll/.

16. https://www.whitehouse.gov/briefing-room/presidential-actions/ 2021/01/20/executive-order-advancing-racial-equity-and-support -for-underserved-communities-through-the-federal-government/.

17. I have documented the Democrats' anti-democratic and anti-constitutional efforts to create a one-party state in my books, *Dark Agenda: The War to Destroy Christian America,* Humanix 2019, and *The Enemy Within: How a Totalitarian Movement Is Destroying America,* Regnery 2021.

18. I have written five books on this subject, including *The Professors, One-Party Classroom, Indoctrination U,* and *Reforming Our Universities.*

19. https://www.discoverthenetworks.org/organizations/1619 -project#resources.

20. https://amgreatness.com/2019/08/16/the-mountebank-left-is -banking-on-you/.

21. https://www.republicanleader.senate.gov/newsroom/remarks/ mcconnell-marks-400th-anniversary-of-our-lands-shameful -history-of-slavery.

22. https://www.youtube.com/results?search_query=how+slavery +ended+thomas+sowell.

Chapter Two

1. https://www.breitbart.com/politics/2022/07/12/elizabeth-warren -calls-to-shut-down-crisis-pregnancy-centers-all-around-the -country/.

2. https://www.wsj.com/articles/the-attacks-on-crisis-pregnancy
-centers-janes-revenge-abortion-roe-v-wade-violence-destroyed
-11655653644; https://www.catholicnewsagency.com/news/
251553/map-vandalism-attacks-continue-at-pro-life-centers
-across-us.

3. https://www.discoverthenetworks.org/individuals/margaret
-sanger; https://www.josephloconte.com/commentary/national
-review-planned-parenthood-and-the-eugenics-movement/.

4. https://www.heritage.org/marriage-and-family/commentary/
new-report-shows-planned-parenthood-raked-15-billion
-taxpayer-funds; https://www.catholicnewsagency.com/news/
46319/planned-parenthood-getting-more-government-funding
-despite-defunding-efforts.

5. https://www.youtube.com/watch?v=RhoFNmMeO8k.

6. https://www.americanadoptions.com/pregnant/waiting_adoptive
_families.

7. https://www.discoverthenetworks.org/organizations/the-2020
-presidential-election-fraud; https://www.politico.com/2020
-election/results/president/.

8. https://ballotpedia.org/Joe_Biden%27s_executive_orders_and
_actions.

9. https://www.cbp.gov/newsroom/stats/southwest-land-border
-encounters.

10. https://www.justice.gov/opa/pr/attorney-general-announces
-zero-tolerance-policy-criminal-illegal-entry.

11. https://abcnews.go.com/Politics/wireStory/ap-fact-check-2020
-democrats-grasp-facts-64615378; https://www.cnn.com/2019/
06/18/politics/alexandria-ocasio-cortez-concentration-camps
-migrants-detention/index.html.

12. https://www.debates.org/voter-education/debate-transcripts/
october-22-2020-debate-transcript/.

13. https://www.nbcnews.com/politics/immigration/trump-says
-he-ll-sign-order-stopping-separation-families-border-n885061.

14. https://www.foxnews.com/politics/biden-migrant-families
-apprehended-border-should-all-be-going-back; https://www
.theblaze.com/news/dhs-secretary-border-crisis-children.

15. https://www.hhs.gov/programs/social-services/unaccompanied
    -children/latest-uc-data-fy2021/index.html.
16. Ibid.
17. https://www.borderreport.com/immigration/cbp-far-fewer
    -migrant-families-unaccompanied-children-came-across-the
    -border-in-october/.
18. https://www.breitbart.com/border/2022/08/05/biden-admin
    -nears-250k-unaccompanied-migrant-child-apprehensions/.
19. https://thehill.com/opinion/immigration/550221-migrant
    -children-suffering-the-unintended-consequences-of-biden
    -policy/.
20. https://www.doctorswithoutborders.org/sites/default/files/
    documents/Doctors%20Without%20Borders_No%20Way%20
    Out%20Report.pdf.
21. https://www.breitbart.com/immigration/2021/06/20/56-house
    -republicans-demand-joe-biden-replace-kamala-harris-failing
    -secure-southern-border/.
22. https://www.breitbart.com/politics/2021/03/01/dhs-sec
    -alejandro-mayorkas-there-no-crisis-border/; https://www
    .foxnews.com/politics/psaki-uses-phrase-crisis-on-the-border
    -during-briefing-then-seems-to-walk-it-back.
23. https://www.kpbs.org/news/2021/mar/30/70-migrant-teens-test
    -positive-covid-19-san-diego-/.
24. https://www.nbcnews.com/politics/immigration/cbp-not-testing
    -migrant-children-covid-border-stations-though-many
    -n1262059.
25. https://www.bbc.com/news/world-us-canada-57149721.
26. https://www.theepochtimes.com/human-trafficking-sexual
    -assaults-key-aspects-of-crisis-on-southern-border_2765383
    .html.
27. https://www.cnn.com/2021/12/09/politics/migrants-dying
    -crossing-us-mexico-border/index.html.
28. https://www.webmd.com/mental-health/addiction/news/
    20220512/drug-overdose-deaths-top-100000-for-first-time.
29. https://guest.house.gov/media/press-releases/guest-introduces
    -resolution-condemn-biden-administration-politicizing-actions.

30. https://www.nytimes.com/2022/07/25/us/migrant-smuggling
-evolution.html; https://www.breitbart.com/economy/2022/07/
26/nytimes-cartels-earn-13-billion-a-year-from-joe-bidens
-welcome-for-migrants/.

31. https://www.foxnews.com/politics/mayorkas-claims-southern
-border-secure-historic-migrant-crisis-rages.

32. https://www.foxnews.com/politics/new-low-biden-approval
-rating-hits-all-time-low-majority-dems-dont-want-run-2024
-poll-shows.

33. Scott Pelley, "60 Minutes interviews the prosecutors of Derek
Chauvin," CBS News, April 26, 2021. Cited in David Horowitz,
I Can't Breathe: How a Racial Hoax Is Killing America, Regnery
2021, p. 60. https://www.linkedin.com/pulse/should-murder
-george-floyd-used-case-study-diversity-charles-m-/?trk=articles
_directory.

34. https://www.commentary.org/articles/christine-rosen/media
-excuse-destructive-violent-riots/.

35. https://www.pewresearch.org/fact-tank/2021/10/27/what-we
-know-about-the-increase-in-u-s-murders-in-2020/.

36. https://www.disastercenter.com/crime/uscrime.htm; https://
www.pewresearch.org/fact-tank/2021/10/27/what-we-know
-about-the-increase-in-u-s-murders-in-2020/; https://
counciloncj.org/2021-year-end-crime-report/.

37. https://www.whitehouse.gov/briefing-room/press-briefings/
2022/05/05/press-briefing-by-press-secretary-jen-psaki-may-5
-2022/; https://www.breitbart.com/politics/2022/05/10/watch
-jen-psaki-says-white-house-encourages-peaceful-protests-out
side-justices-homes/.

38. David Horowitz and John Perazzo, *Internal Radical Service*,
Ch. 2: "Zuckerberg's Tax-Exempt Election Machine," 2022.

39. https://imprimis.hillsdale.edu/critical-race-theory-fight/.

40. https://www.cnn.com/2022/03/30/politics/clinton-dnc-steele
-dossier-fusion-gps/index.html; https://www.washingtonpost.com/
world/national-security/clinton-campaign-dnc-paid-for-research
-that-led-to-russia-dossier/2017/10/24/226fabf0-b8e4-11e7-a908
-a3470754bbb9_story.html; https://nypost.com/2022/04/09/
america-is-still-paying-the-price-for-hillary-clintons-treachery/.

41. https://thehill.com/homenews/senate/536364-kaine-eyes-next
-week-to-file-trump-censure-aiming-to-bar-him-from-future/.

42. https://www.washingtontimes.com/news/2021/feb/18/
democrats-bill-would-ban-trumps-name-us-buildings-/.

43. Ibid.

44. https://www.newsweek.com/liz-cheney-voted-donald-trump-93
-percent-congress-1734186; https://thehill.com/homenews/
campaign/3602899-trump-eyes-big-prize-in-taking-down
-cheney/; and https://projects.fivethirtyeight.com/congress-trump
-score/liz-cheney/.

45. https://thehill.com/homenews/house/3542366-liz-cheney
-trump-a-domestic-threat-that-we-have-never-faced-before/.

46. https://nypost.com/2022/03/01/jan-6-capitol-rioter-dies-by
-suicide-because-of-broken-heart-over-case/; https://www
.newsweek.com/georgia-man-arrested-pro-trump-capitol-riot
-dies-suicide-1561005.

47. https://thehill.com/regulation/court-battles/3598072-former
-virginia-police-officer-sentenced-to-more-than-7-years-for-role
-on-jan-6/.

48. https://apnews.com/article/election-2020-joe-biden-donald-
trump-capitol-siege-media-e79eb5164613d6718e9f4502eb471f27.

49. https://www.npr.org/2021/02/10/966396848/read-trumps-jan-6
-speech-a-key-part-of-impeachment-trial.

50. https://justthenews.com/government/congress/trump-gave
-explicit-order-about-jan-6-rally-make-sure-it-was-safe-event
-dod.

51. https://meaww.com/benjamin-phillips-death-capitol-riots
-trumparoo-donald-trump-died-stroke-pennsylvania-ex-wife
-kids.

52. Ibid.

53. https://www.americanthinker.com/blog/2021/02/biden_lies_
about_capitol_police_officer_brian_sicknicks_death.html.

54. https://www.pbs.org/newshour/politics/watch-live-funeral-for
-capitol-police-officer-brian-sicknick.

55. https://www.americanthinker.com/blog/2021/02/biden_lies_
about_capitol_police_officer_brian_sicknicks_death.html.

56. https://www.washingtonexaminer.com/news/house/jan-6
    -committee-chairman-officers-lost-lives-capitol-riot; https://
    www.dailymail.co.uk/news/article-9129929/U-S-Capitol-police
    -officer-died-violent-assault-loved-job.html.

57. https://www.americanthinker.com/blog/2022/01/ashli_babbitts_
    murderer_exonerated_in_disgraceful_official_investigation.html.

58. https://www.realclearinvestigations.com/articles/2022/01/06/
    capitol_police_officer_who_shot_ashli_babbitt_refused_to_
    answer_investigators_questions_810720.html#!.

Chapter Three

1. Mark Rudd, *Underground: My Life with SDS and the Weathermen*,
   Kindle edition, loc. 3069.

2. Rudd, op. cit. loc. 3078.

3. Peter Collier and David Horowitz, *Destructive Generation*, 1989,
   p. 94.

4. https://law.justia.com/cases/california/court-of-appeal/3d/61/
   102.html.

5. ttps://slate.com/news-and-politics/2001/08/radical-chic
   -resurgent.html; https://www.chicagomag.com/chicago
   -magazine/may-1993/rebel-without-a-pause/.

6. Ibid.

7. Op. cit., Frontispiece.

8. https://books.google.com/books?id=WEmN1ZKrYpsC&pg
   =PA222&lpg=#v=onepage&q&f=false.

9. Rudd, op. cit., *Underground*, Kindle edition, loc. 3100.

10. David Horowitz, *Radical Son*, 1997 Part 5. Bryan Burrough, *Days
    of Rage*.

11. https://acleddata.com/acleddatanew/wp-content/uploads/
    2020/09/ACLED_USDataReview_Sum2020_SeptWebPDF.pdf.

12. https://www.youtube.com/watch?v=Wp7hl2x2dDY&t=616s.

13. Bryan Burrough, *Days of Rage: America's Radical Underground,
    the FBI, and the Forgotten Age of Revolutionary Violence*, 2015.

14. Ibid.

15. https://books.google.com/books?id=Dr0UIZJw58YC&pg
    =PA390&lpg=PA390&dq=#v=onepage&q&f=false.

16. https://files.libcom.org/files/Ebook.DownAppz.com%20-%20 Underground_%20My%20Life%20with%20SDS%20and%20the %20Weathermen.pdf.

17. https://www.vanityfair.com/culture/2015/03/weather -underground-bomb-guru-burrough-excerpt.

18. Rudd, *Underground*, op. cit., Kindle edition, loc. 3176.

19. Rudd, *Underground*, op. cit., Kindle edition, loc. 3149.

20. https://www.discoverthenetworks.org/individuals/noel-ignatiev.

21. https://www.discoverthenetworks.org/organizations/race -traitor-journal-of-the-new-abolitionism-rt.

22. *New York Times*, June 15, 1969, p. 20.

23. https://www.amazon.com/Dont-Need-Weatherman-Which-Blows/ dp/1453726756.

24. https://twitter.com/potus/status/1354221331605319681.

25. https://www.discoverthenetworks.org/individuals/antonio -gramsci.

26. Bullock, Alan; Trombley, Stephen, Editors (1999), *The New Fontana Dictionary of Modern Thought*, Third Edition, pp. 387–88.

27. https://www.cnsnews.com/commentary/dr-paul-kengor/how -obama-made-good-his-promise-fundamentally-transform -united-states.

28. John Perazzo, "The Ugly Racism of 'Whiteness Studies' Programs," FrontPageMag.com https://www.frontpagemag.com/fpm/ 263671/ugly-racism-whiteness-studies-programs-john-perazzo.

29. https://www.google.com/search?client=firefox-b-1-d&q =abolition+of+whiteness.

30. https://www.lohud.com/story/news/local/rockland/nyack/ 2019/04/17/brinks-judith-clark-granted-parole-1981-robbery -murders/3494841002/.

31. https://www.discoverthenetworks.org/individuals/chesa-boudin.

32. https://www.foxnews.com/us/columbias-cons-ivy-league-social -work-program-run-by-team-of-former-prisoners.

33. https://www.theepochtimes.com/college-professors-95-times -more-likely-to-donate-to-democrats-than-republicans-study _3217738.html?slsuccess=1.

34. https://www.nas.org/academic-questions/31/2/homogenous_ the_political_affiliations_of_elite_liberal_arts_college_faculty.

35. https://www.foxnews.com/us/harvard-university-student
    -newspaper-survey-graduates-finds-results.
36. https://townhall.com/columnists/carlhorowitz/2007/07/14/
    corporate-diversity-training-n1097283.
37. https://www.ourdocuments.gov/doc.php?flash=false&doc=97
    &page=transcript.
38. https://www.archives.gov/founding-docs/constitution-transcript.
39. https://www.discoverthenetworks.org/organizations/origins
    -history-evolution-of-affirmative-action.
40. https://nypost.com/2012/05/22/stop-frisk-facts/.
41. Thomas Sowell, *Conquests and Cultures* (New York: Basic
    Books), 1998, section titled "The Africans: Slavery, pp. 109–112;
    Dinesh D'Souza, *The End of Racism* (New York: The Free Press),
    1995, pp. 71–74.
42. https://www.digitalhistory.uh.edu/era.cfm?eraid=7&smtid=1.
43. https://www.lubbockonline.com/story/opinion/columns/
    2014/06/23/williams-call-slavery-reparations-simply-another
    -hustle/15035521007/.
44. https://www.pbs.org/wnet/african-americans-many-rivers-to
    -cross/history/how-many-slaves-landed-in-the-us/.
45. https://www.lubbockonline.com/story/opinion/columns/2014/
    06/23/williams-call-slavery-reparations-simply-another-hustle/
    15035521007/.
46. Thomas Sowell, *Black Rednecks and White Liberals* (San
    Francisco: Encounter Books, 2005), See Chapter 3: "The Real
    History of Slavery."
47. https://qz.com/africa/1333946/global-slavery-index-africa-has
    -the-highest-rate-of-modern-day-slavery-in-the-world/.
48. https://insights.som.yale.edu/insights/yale-study-finds-twice-as
    -many-undocumented-immigrants-as-previous-estimates;
    https://www.dailywire.com/news/9-things-you-need-know
    -about-illegal-immigration-aaron-bandler; https://www
    .washingtonexaminer.com/illegal-immigrants-responsible-for
    -almost-three-fourths-of-federal-drug-possession-sentences-in
    -2014; https://immigration.procon.org/questions/does-illegal
    -immigration-relate-to-higher-crime-incidence/#quote-1275;
    https://thehill.com/latino/331619-doj-releases-data-on

-incarceration-rates-of-illegal-immigrants; https://thehill.com/
opinion/immigration/407312-one-in-five-us-prison-inmates-is
-a-criminal-alien.

49. https://dailycaller.com/2019/01/17/trump-wall-tucker-guest
-brown/.

50. https://www.thereligionofpeace.com/.

51. https://www.learningforjustice.org/magazine/fall-2018/what-is
-white-privilege-really.

52. https://nypost.com/2012/05/22/stop-frisk-facts/; https://www
.city-journal.org/html/why-cops-stop-and-frisk-so-many-blacks
-10216.html; https://nypost.com/2009/05/19/face-facts-on
-frisks/.

53. https://www.aclu.org/news/criminal-law-reform/stop-and-frisks
-plummeted-under-new-york-mayor.

54. https://www.city-journal.org/html/distorting-truth-about-crime
-and-race-10730.html.

55. Ibid.

56. https://www.ojp.gov/pdffiles1/nij/248588.pdf.

57. https://www.city-journal.org/html/distorting-truth-about-crime
-and-race-10730.html.

58. https://www.nyclu.org/en/stop-and-frisk-data.

59. https://www.learningforjustice.org/magazine/fall-2018/what-is
-white-privilege-really.

60. https://www.celebritynetworth.com/richest-celebrities/actors/
oprah-net-worth/.

61. https://ifstudies.org/blog/family-breakdown-and-americas
-welfare-system.

62. https://www.ceousa.org/2020/02/26/percentage-of-births-to
-unmarried-women/; https://www.heartland.org/publications
-resources/publications/illegitimacy-ratio-declining.

63. https://www.ramseysolutions.com/retirement/millionaire
-myth-busters.

64. https://www.discoverthenetworks.org/organizations/research
-on-affirmative-action-in-academia#resources.

Chapter Four

1. https://www.politico.eu/article/
   tony-blair-withdrawal-from-afghanistan-imbecilic-taliban/.
2. https://horowitzfreedomcenterstore.org/products/disloyal.
3. Daniel Greenfield, *How Obama and Biden Destroyed the Greatest Military the World Has Ever Seen*, Frontpagemag.com 2022, p. 36.
4. John Perazzo, Mark Tapson & David Horowitz, "Betraying America," in Daniel Greenfield, *Disloyal: How the Military Brass is Betraying Our Country*, Frontpagemag.com, 2021.
5. https://www.factcheck.org/2021/08/timeline-of-u-s-withdrawal
   -from-afghanistan/.
6. https://edition.cnn.com/2021/02/03/politics/pentagon-stand
   -down-domestic-extremism-military/index.html.
7. https://sgp.fas.org/crs/natsec/RL32492.pdf.
8. https://www.amazon.com/Irresistible-Revolution-Marxisms
   -Conquest-Unmaking-ebook/dp/B0952DZ46D/ref=.
9. Ibid.
10. https://www.military.com/daily-news/2021/05/20/space-force
    -co-fired-over-comments-about-marxism-military-now-subject
    -of-ig-probe.html.
11. https://books.google.com/books?id=D-IuEAAAQBAJ&pg
    =PT142&lpg=PT142&dq=#v=onepage&q&f=false.
12. https://www.amazon.com/You-Want-Talk-About-Race-ebook/
    dp/B07QBNKJTZ/ref=.
13. https://www.amazon.com/Irresistible-Revolution-Marxisms
    -Conquest-Unmaking-ebook/dp/B0952DZ46D/ref=.
14. https://www.nytimes.com/2021/05/12/us/politics/domestic
    -terror-white-supremacists.html.
15. https://www.city-journal.org/democratic-candidates-racism
    -crime. When the Bureau of Justice Statistics released its 2018 survey of criminal victimization, it showed there were 593,598 interracial violent victimizations (excluding homicide) between blacks and whites, including white-on-black and black-on-white attacks. Blacks committed 537,204 of those interracial felonies, or 90 percent, and whites committed 56,394 of them, or less than

10 percent. That ratio is becoming more skewed, despite the Democratic claim of Trump-inspired white violence. In 2012 and 2013, blacks committed 85 percent of all interracial victimizations between blacks and whites; whites committed 15 percent. From 2015 to 2018, the total number of white victims and the incidence of white victimization have grown as well. Blacks are also overrepresented among perpetrators of hate crimes—by 50 percent—according to the most recent Department of Justice data from 2017; whites are underrepresented by 24 percent. This is particularly true for anti-gay and anti-Semitic hate crimes.

16. Wikipedia, Siad Barre, note 42.
17. Wikipedia, Siad Barre, note 47.
18. Wikipedia, Siad Barre, note 48.
19. https://www.discoverthenetworks.org/individuals/ilhan-omar.
20. Ibid.
21. https://www.cfr.org/timeline/al-shabab.
22. https://www.mprnews.org/story/2015/04/29/fears-of-spying -intensify-after-twin-cities-terror-arrests.
23. Weingarten, Benjamin. *American Ingrate: Ilhan Omar and the Progressive-Islamist Takeover of the Democratic Party*, Kindle edition p. 32.
24. https://www.dailywire.com/news/ilhan-omars-district-terrorist -recruitment-capital-ryan-saavedra.
25. Discover the Networks, Ilhan Omar, www.discoverthenetworks.org.
26. Ibid.
27. Discover the Networks, www.discoverthenetworks.org.
28. https://www.factcheck.org/2019/04/rep-ilhan-omars-9-11 -comments-in-context/.
29. https://www.humanrightsfirst.org/blog/islam-peace-let-s -remember-george-w-bush-s-words-after-911.
30. https://ucr.fbi.gov/hate-crime/2019/topic-pages/tables/table-1 .xls.
31. https://www.discoverthenetworks.org/organizations/muslim -students-association-of-the-us-and-canada-msa; https:// www.discoverthenetworks.org/organizations/students-for -justice-in-palestine-sjp.

32. https://www.dailywire.com/news/dem-candidate-ilhan-omar
-defending-tweet-evil-frank-camp.

33. https://twitter.com/RashidaTlaib/status/1402976108845449218.

34. https://www.investigativeproject.org/7892/aoc-tlaib-met-with
-amp-members-during-palestine.

35. https://www.discoverthenetworks.org/organizations/american
-muslims-for-palestine-amp; https://www.globalmbwatch.com/
american-muslims-for-palestine/.

36. https://freebeacon.com/politics/omar-criticism-of-tlaib-part-of
-efforts-to-eliminate-the-public-voice-of-muslims/.

37. https://www.jewishvirtuallibrary.org/haj-amin-al-husseini.

38. https://www.investigativeproject.org/7892/aoc-tlaib-met-with
-amp-members-during-palestine.

39. https://www.meforum.org/58206/new-islamist-lobby.

40. Ibid.

41. https://www.foxnews.com/politics/israel-iron-dome-house
-members-vote-against-funding.

42. https://www.amazon.com/Unholy-Alliance-Radical-Islam
-American/dp/B0073MJRS4/ref=sr_1_1.

43. https://www.newsweek.com/nancy-pelosi-defends-ilhan
-omar-against-trump-911-1395404.

44. https://twitter.com/berniesanders/status/1116855482038272000.

45. https://twitter.com/ewarren/status/1116859387199533057?lang=en.

46. "In a final resolution, we would not see the presence of a single
Israeli—civilian or soldier—on our lands," Abbas told a group of
reporters. https://www.israelnationalnews.com/news/170404.

47. https://www.thereligionofpeace.com/.

48. https://www.danielpipes.org/comments/23648.

49. https://quran.com/47/4?translations=21,85,95,17,18,19,20,22,84,101.

50. https://www.jpost.com/opinion/no-holds-barred-the-mysterious
-motivation-of-jewish-leaders-who-visit-hamass-funders-in
-qatar-516998.

51. https://www.foxnews.com/opinion/qanta-ahmed-ilhan-omar-is
-a-disgrace-to-islam-and-doesnt-represent-my-muslim-religion.

52. Ibid.

53. https://www.nytimes.com/2019/02/11/opinion/ilhan-omar
-antisemitism.html.

54. Ibid.

55. Cited in Weingarten, Benjamin. *American Ingrate: Ilhan Omar and the Progressive-Islamist Takeover of the Democratic Party,* Bombardier Books, p. 129.

56. Ibid.

57. https://www.investigativeproject.org/7855/pelosi-caves-to -anti-semites-and-supporters.

58. https://www.youtube.com/watch?v=gWEQ9hhXQF.

59. https://www.nytimes.com/1997/05/06/world/palestinians-face -death-for-selling-land-to-jews.html.

60. Ibram X. Kendi, *How to Be an Antiracist,* Kindle Edition loc. 335.

61. Benjamin Weingarten, *American Ingrate,* Kindle Edition, loc 1042.

Chapter Five

1. https://api.discoverthenetworks.org/wp-content/uploads/2021/ 01/TrumpvBiden4PDF.pdf.

2. https://www.discoverthenetworks.org/organizations/americas -asylum-laws-the-border-crisis.

3. https://api.discoverthenetworks.org/wp-content/uploads/2021/ 01/TrumpvBiden4PDF.pdf.

4. https://nypost.com/2021/01/15/aoc-proposes-funding-to -deprogram-white-supremacists/.

5. https://thehill.com/homenews/house/487699-clyburn-calls -trump-a-racist-warns-us-could-go-the-way-of-germany-in-the -1930s.

6. https://en.wikipedia.org/wiki/The_Moral_Landscape.

7. https://video.search.yahoo.com/yhs/search?fr=yhs-ima -tabitab&ei=UTF-8&hsimp=yhs-tabitab&hspart=ima&p=sam +harris+on+getting+trump&type=q3080_D3KZN_ext_bcrq #id=3&vid=bd9c3bf87019cf89e55d5a04e5693ecf&action=click.

8. https://search.yahoo.com/yhs/search?hspart=mnet&hsimp=yhs -001&type=type9097303-spa-4056-84481&param1=4056&para m2=84481&p=uc.

9. https://covid.podclips.com/c/A4Ivo4.

10. https://www.nbcnews.com/politics/white-house/federal-court
    -approves-25-million-trump-university-settlement-n845181;
    https://www.politico.com/story/2016/06/trump-university
    -success-stories-223785.
11. https://covid.podclips.com/c/A4Ivo4.
12. https://nypost.com/2022/05/18/justice-coming-for-dirty-51
    -hunter-biden-laptop-liars/.
13. https://www.discoverthenetworks.org/organizations/the-2020
    -presidential-election-fraud.
14. https://covid.podclips.com/c/A4Ivo4.
15. https://nypost.com/2022/08/19/sam-harris-defends-silencing
    -the-post-on-hunter-biden/.
16. Dean Obeidallah, "Elie Mystal: Our Constitution is 'actually
    trash'—but the Supreme Court can be fixed." *Salon*, March 23,
    2022.
17. F.A. Hayek, *The Mirage of Social Justice*, Chicago: University of
    Chicago Press, 1976.
18. https://www.heritage.org/welfare/report/understanding-the
    -hidden-11-trillion-welfare-system-and-how-reform-it.
19. https://www.wsj.com/articles/coronavirus-relief-often-pays
    -workers-more-than-work-11588066200.
20. https://twitter.com/forbes/status/1391811314146844674?lang
    =en.
21. https://thehill.com/homenews/administration/597675-biden
    -blames-putins-price-hike-for-high-inflation/.
22. https://www.newson6.com/story/6242d90b42bd707e5c32ddd0/
    bidens-2023-budget-request-gives-boost-to-nasas-artemis
    -moon-program; https://airandspace.si.edu/stories/editorial/
    stephanie-wilson-to-the-moon.
23. https://www.discoverthenetworks.org/organizations/radical
    -prosecutors.
24. https://nypost.com/2020/08/11/black-lives-matter-organizer
    -calls-chicago-looting-reparation/.
25. https://progressives.house.gov/caucus-members.
26. https://www.discoverthenetworks.org/individuals/pramila
    -jayapal.

27. https://www.mercatus.org/publications/education-policy/
reevaluating-effects-federal-financing-higher-education.

28. https://www.heritage.org/education/commentary/the-high
-cost-free-college-tuition; https://www.pewresearch.org/
fact-tank/2021/08/11/democrats-overwhelmingly-favor-free
-college-tuition-while-republicans-are-divided-by-age
-education/; https://www.politico.com/newsletters/weekly
-education/2021/09/20/democrats-hammer-out-details-of-free
-community-college-plan-797684; https://www.vox.com/2019/
6/24/18677785/democrats-free-college-sanders-warren-biden.

29. https://www.thedailybeast.com/when-iran-took-americans
-hostage-bernie-backed-irans-defenders.

30. https://www.celebritynetworth.com/richest-politicians/
democrats/bernie-sanders-net-worth/.

31. https://www.cnn.com/2019/03/14/politics/kfile-bernie
-nationalization/index.html.

32. https://www.discoverthenetworks.org/individuals/bernie-sanders.

33. https://twitter.com/TerriJRickman/status/1511365234556121089.

34. https://www.discoverthenetworks.org/individuals/bernie-sanders.

35. https://www.discoverthenetworks.org/individuals/stokely
-carmichael-aka-kwame-ture.

36. https://freerepublic.com/focus/bloggers/3393818/posts.

37. https://www.discoverthenetworks.org/individuals/bernie-sanders.

38. https://www.independent.co.uk/arts-entertainment/tv/news/
elon-musk-billionaire-joe-rogan-interview-grimes-baby-selling
-house-possessions-a9504691.html; https://twitter.com/
elonmusk/status/1256239554148724737?lang=en.

39. https://www.celebritynetworth.com/richest-celebrities/rock-stars/
bob-dylan-net-worth/; https://americansongwriter.com/eric
-claptons-net-worth-and-legacy-from-cocaine-to-this-has
-gotta-stop/.

40. https://hoopshype.com/salaries/golden_state_warriors/.

41. https://www.govtrack.us/congress/votes/103-1994/h416; https://
www.govtrack.us/congress/votes/103-1994/s295.

42. https://www.foxnews.com/media/bill-maher-joe-rogan
-democrats-midterms-no-common-sense.

43. https://www.whitehouse.gov/briefing-room/presidential-actions/
    2021/01/20/executive-order-advancing-racial-equity-and-support
    -for-underserved-communities-through-the-federal-government/.

44. https://www.borderreport.com/hot-topics/immigration/migrant
    -encounters-top-2-million-in-calendar-year-2021-on-pace-for
    -repeat-in-2022/.

45. https://www.washingtonexaminer.com/news/conservatives
    -point-out-that-princeton-study-on-protests-reveals-violence
    -was-found-at-hundreds-of-demonstrations.

46. http://www.thefamuanonline.com/2021/03/13/black-lives-matter
    -collects-almost-100-million-in-donations/.

47. https://www.discoverthenetworks.org/organizations/blms-close
    -ties-to-the-democratic-party; https://archives.frontpagemag.com/
    fpm/dems-officially-endorse-anti-cop-blacklivesmatter
    -matthew-vadum/.

48. https://www.discoverthenetworks.org/individuals/alicia-garza;
    https://www.discoverthenetworks.org/individuals/patrisse
    -cullors; https://www.discoverthenetworks.org/individuals/opal
    -tometi.

49. https://www.discoverthenetworks.org/organizations/gender-pay
    -gap; https://www.dailywire.com/news/7-facts-show-women
    -are-not-victims-pay-amanda-prestigiacomo.

50. https://www.mckinsey.com/industries/financial-services/our
    -insights/women-as-the-next-wave-of-growth-in-us-wealth
    -management.

51. https://www.statista.com/statistics/200476/us-poverty-rate-by
    -ethnic-group/.

52. https://www.archives.gov/research/african-americans/
    migrations/great-migration#.

53. Stephan Thernstrom and Abigail Thernstrom, America in Black
    and White (New York: Simon & Schuster, 1997), pp. 81–82.

54. Ibid.

55. Thomas Sowell, The Economics and Politics of Race (New York:
    Quill, 1983), pp. 190–191.

56. https://go.gale.com/ps/i.do?id=GALE%7CA675267752&sid
    =googleScholar&v=2.1&it=r&linkaccess=abs&issn=10861653&p

=AONE&sw=w&userGroupName=nysl_oweb&isGeoAuthType
=true.

57. Tony Snow, "Blacks Should Not Abandon King's Dream,"
Conservative Chronicle (September 7, 1994), p. 28; Walter E.
Williams, "White People Are Divine," More Liberty Means Less
Government (Stanford: Hoover Institution Press, 1999), p. 6.

58. https://www.census.gov/content/dam/Census/library/
publications/2020/demo/p60-270.pdf (see Table B2, p. 58).

59. https://www.ceousa.org/2020/02/26/percentage-of-births-to
-unmarried-women/.

60. David Horowitz, Blitz: Trump Will Smash the Left and Win,
2020, p. 8.

61. Ibid.

62. Horowitz, op. cit., p. 9.

63. https://nypost.com/2020/08/25/nancy-pelosi-trump-gop
-lawmakers-are-enemies-of-the-state/.

ACKNOWLEDGMENTS

I was supported throughout the writing of this book by the tireless dedication of Mike Finch, president of the David Horowitz Freedom Center, the research skills of John Perazzo and Mike Bauer, the devotion of my Executive Assistant, Elizabeth Ruiz and my field director Lonny Leitner, the editorial wisdom of Jamie Glazov, the marketing skills of Todd Snider and the brilliance of the Center's writers—Robert Spencer, Daniel Greenfield, Mark Tapson, Bruce Thornton, Bruce Bawer, and others too numerous to mention. Most of the staff have been working at the Center for 20 years, to which I attribute their understanding of the importance of our mission and the quality of their character.

I also want to thank President Trump, Mark Levin, Larry Elder, Charlie Kirk, Pete Hegseth, Chris Salcedo, Eric Metaxas, and our media rep, Sandy Frazier, who have brought wider attention to our work.

Last, but not least, I want to pay respect to an unsung hero in the battle to save America, Chris Ruddy, founder of Newsmax, without whose support my books would not have been successful and my words would not have reached the millions of readers that they have.

INDEX

Abbas, Mahmoud, 88
ABC, 62
Abortion, 27
Affirmative action, 56–57
Afghanistan, 73–75, 77, 101
Africa and Africans, 19, 21,
    63–64, 78–79, 132
Ahmed, Qanta, 89–90
AIPAC, 90
Al-Husseini, Haj Amin, 86
Ali, Muhammad, 98
Al-Jazeera TV, 81, 83
Allen, Theodore, 54
Al-Qaeda, 73, 74, 80, 88
Al-Qaradawi, Yousuf, 88–89
Al-Shabab, 80
Al-Zawahiri, Ayman, 80
Amazon, 125
Amendments, constitutional, 9
American Ingrate (Weingarten), 91
American Israel Public Affairs
    Committee (AIPAC), 90
American Muslims for Palestine
    (AMP), 79, 84–86
"Amerikkka," 49, 54, 56
Amnesty International, 79
Anti-law-enforcement
    campaigns, 34–35 (*See
    also* Black Lives Matter)

Anti-Semitism, 84, 89–92, 117,
    120
Anti-war movement, 7–9
Anti-white racism, 47–50,
    53–69, 74–75, 78, 80–82,
    87, 92, 111, 117, 118, 120,
    131, 132, 135–136
AOC (*see* Ocasio-Cortez,
    Alexandria)
Apple, 77, 121–122
Arlington National Cemetery,
    39, 43
Asians, 69
Austin, Lloyd, 73–74, 76
Ayers, Billy, 52–53, 59

Babbitt, Ashli, 44
Barre, Siad, 78–79
Benin, 19
Biden, Hunter, 102, 104, 105
Biden, Joe, 12, 14, 28–34, 36, 41,
    43, 56, 57, 73, 100–102,
    104–105, 114, 115, 127,
    128, 135
Bin Laden, Osama, 80, 101
Bin Laden family, 83
Binh, Nguyen Thi, 7, 8
Birth control, 23
Black Liberation Army, 59

Black Lives Matter, 13, 33–34, 52, 56, 74, 76, 129, 135
Black Panthers, 48, 50–51, 54, 55
"Black Power," 120
Blacks:
    and anti-white racism, 78, 120
    in Congress, 87, 88, 91–93
    and the Constitution, 12, 62
    as crime victims, 33–35, 47, 51, 59, 66
    as "marginalized" group, 68–69, 73, 129–131
    and Marxist race theory, 36, 48, 50, 51, 61, 115, 116, 129, 136
    and poverty, 67, 93, 112–113, 132–135
    and slavery, 19–21, 63–64, 132–133
    and "Stop and Frisk," 65–66
    wealth accumulation by, 66–67, 133–134
Blair, Tony, 73
Bolshevism, 6
Boudin, Kathy, 59–60
"Bourgeois" morality, 6
Boycott, Divestment and Sanctions Movement, 84, 85
Brown, Ketanji Jackson, 36–37
Bush, Cori, 78
Bush, George W., 83
Byrd, Michael, 44

CAIR, 79, 82–83
Cambodia, 7–8
Capitalism, 57, 115, 124–125
Capitol protest (see January 6th Capitol protest)
Carmichael, Stokely, 120
Carrizo Springs, Tex., 31
Castro, Fidel, 1, 7, 48
CBS, 62

Center for the Study of White American Culture, 58
Centers for Disease Control, 35
Central America, 30
Central Intelligence Agency (CIA), 102
Charlottesville riot, 103
Chauvin, Derek, 33
Cheney, Liz, 39–40
Chicago, Ill., 48
"Children in cages" controversy, 28, 29
China, 31, 101, 107, 136
Chomsky, Noam, 8
Christians and Christianity, 20, 80, 88, 139, 140
CIA (Central Intelligence Agency), 102
Citizenship, 67–68
Civil Rights Act of 1964, 56, 133
Civil rights movement, 130
Civil War, 19, 21
Clapton, Eric, 126
Class, 6
Cleaver, Eldridge, 48
Clinton, Bill, 80, 98, 127
Clinton, Hillary, 38, 97–99
Clyburn, James, 100
CNN, 62
Cold War, 117
Colleges and universities, 7, 15, 47, 51, 58, 60–63, 68, 74–75, 85, 111, 112, 117, 135
Columbia School of Social Work, 60
Columbia Teachers College, 59
Columbia University, 48
Combs, Sean "P. Diddy," 67
Communists and communism, 4, 7–10, 47, 50, 54, 57, 59, 78, 79, 101, 102, 109, 111, 116–118

Compromise, 16–17
Confederacy, 19, 38–39
Confinity, 123
Congress, 10–11, 39, 43, 80–82,
    87, 117, 127, 131 (*See also*
    House of Representatives;
    Senate)
Congressional Black Caucus, 91
Conservatives and
    conservatism, 5, 16–18,
    36, 60–61, 65, 81, 104, 109,
    116, 127, 128, 136
Constitution, 3, 5–6, 9, 10–12,
    15, 16, 20, 35–38, 62, 75,
    76, 97, 111, 112, 115–116
Council on Foreign Relations, 89
COVID-19 pandemic, 31, 125
Crime, 13, 20, 25, 28, 32–37,
    50–52, 56, 58, 59–60, 66,
    68, 78, 84, 110–112, 116,
    117, 127–128, 133, 136
Crime Bill (1994), 127–128
Criminal justice system, 128
Critical Race Theory, 15, 36–37,
    74
Critical Race Theory (Delgado), 71
Cuba, 7, 136
Cultural hegemony, 57
Cultural Marxism, 15–16, 57–58
Cultural Revolution, 107
Curry, Steph, 126

"Days of Rage," 48, 52
Declaration of Independence,
    118
Deferred Action for Childhood
    Arrivals (DACA), 11–12
Deferred Action for Parents of
    Americans and Lawful
    Permanent Residents
    (DAPA), 12
"Defund the Police," 13, 56,
    110–111

Delgado, Richard, 71
Democracy(-ies), 11, 17, 35, 37,
    38, 41, 97, 99, 103–106,
    109, 110, 112
Democratic National
    Committee, 38, 80
Democrats and Democrat Party,
    3, 5, 13–15, 17, 18, 20,
    26, 28–30, 32–36, 38–44,
    60, 62–65, 80, 81, 86–91,
    97–100, 104, 112–116,
    118, 129, 135–136
Department of Defense
    (Pentagon), 7, 41, 52,
    73–74, 76
Department of Health and
    Human Services, 30, 31
Department of Homeland
    Security, 29
Department of Justice, 36
Detroit News, 135
The Devils (Dostoevsky), 49
Devine, Miranda, 104
DiAngelo, Robin, 92
Director of National Intelligence
    (DNI), 102
"Diversity, equity, and inclusion"
    programs, 61, 74–75, 92
"Diversity" programs, 61
DNI (Director of National
    Intelligence), 102
Doctors Without Borders, 30
Dohrn, Bernardine, 48–50, 52,
    53, 59
Domestic terrorism, 20, 25, 52,
    76–78
Dostoevsky, Fyodor, 49
Drug trade, 31
Due process, 10
Dylan, Bob, 126

Election of 2016, 14, 37, 38, 97,
    98, 134–135

Election of 2020, 40, 97, 98, 104, 106, 119
Electoral College, 17, 110
Electric cars, 123–124
Ellison, Keith, 33, 80
Emancipation Proclamation, 20
"The end justifies the means," 6, 7
The End of Faith and the Moral Landscape (Harris), 100
England, 64
Equal Pay for Equal Work Act (1963), 131
"Equity" policies, 14, 57, 61, 74–75, 92, 116, 128
Eugenics, 26–27
Executive orders, 28

Faith, 3
Family, 133, 136, 139
Federal Bureau of Investigation (FBI), 51, 84, 104
Federal system, 17–18
Fentanyl, 31, 33, 56
First Amendment, 18
Flint, Mich., 47, 50, 54
Flint War Council, 52
Floyd, George, 33, 35, 51, 56
Fonda, Jane, 7
Ford, Harold, 128
Fort Dix, 53
The Forward, 90
Fossil fuels, 113
Founders, 6, 11, 16–17, 86, 109–110, 140
Fourteenth Amendment, 38–39
Freedom, faith in, 3
Fudge, Marcia, 91
Fugitive Days (Ayers), 52–53

Gallup, 14
Garland, Merrick, 77
Gaza, 84–86, 117

Geneva Convention, 87
Ghana, 19
Gilbert, Chesa, 59
Gilbert, David, 59
God, 89, 100, 111, 118
Golden State Warriors, 126
Google, 77
Gramsci, Antonio, 57
Great Society, 133
Greenfield, David, 74
Guevara, Che, 48

Hamas, 79, 82, 84–88, 91
Harris, Kamala, 30, 103
Harris, Sam, 30, 100–105
Harvard Crimson, 60–61
Harvard Law School, 111
Harvard University, 54, 60–61
Hatzair, Hashomer, 120–121
Hayden, Tom, 7
Hayek, Friedrich, 112
Hazan, Ya'akov, 120–121
Hispanic Americans, 32–33, 65, 66
Hitchcock, Jeff, 58
Hitler, Adolf, 8, 86, 100, 115
Ho Chi Minh, 48
Hobsbawm, Eric, 116
Holocaust, 8, 85, 89
Homeland Security, 32, 77
House Foreign Affairs Committee, 82, 84
House of Representatives, 39, 40, 44, 78, 82, 84, 86–88, 91, 92, 100, 131
House Select Committee to Investigate the January 6th Attack on the United States Capitol, 40–41, 43–44
How to Be an Anti-Racist (Xendi), 93
Human Rights Watch, 79

Ideological racism, 91–93
Ideologies, 128
IfNotNow, 91
Ignatiev, Noel, 54
Immigrants (immigration),
	10–12, 25, 28–33, 63,
	67–68, 79, 81
Indochina, 7–8
Inflation, 113–115
Inflation Reduction Act, 114
"Inherited wealth," 67
Intercontinental Ballistic
	Missiles (ICBMs), 123
The Invention of the White Race
	(Allen), 54
Iran, 79, 82, 85, 87, 118
Iraq, 82
Iron Dome missile defense
	system, 87
Irresistible Revolution
	(Lohmeier), 75
ISIS, 88
Islamic terrorism, 64, 73, 74,
	79–90, 117 (*See also* 9/11
	terrorist attacks)
Islamism, 86, 89, 90
Islamist-Progressive Alliance,
	86
Islamofascism, 118
"Islamophobia," 81, 91, 99
Israel, 84–88, 90, 92–93, 99, 118,
	120

Jacobs, John "J. J.," 49, 53, 54
January 6th Capitol protest,
	39–44, 73, 98
Jayapal, Pramila, 117
Jefferson, Thomas, 19
Jesus Christ, 140
Jews and Judaism, 8, 16, 69, 80,
	84–89, 92, 93, 117, 120,
	130, 132
Jihad, 79, 86, 87, 89

Jim Crow, 75
Jobs, Steve, 121–122, 125
Judeo-Christian religions,
	139–140
Justice Democrats, 91
Justice Department, 56

Kaine, Tim, 39
Kavanaugh, Brett, 36
Kenya, 79
King, Martin Luther, 120
Ku Klux Klan, 91, 92

Learning for Justice, 65, 66
Leftists and the left, 3, 6, 8–10,
	12, 15, 18, 21, 25–26, 34,
	50–51, 55–57, 60–69,
	73, 74, 76, 91, 93, 97, 99,
	102, 103, 105, 116, 121,
	124–125, 135
Lenin, Vladimir, 48
Liberty, 139
Lincoln, Abraham, 19
Lohmeier, Matt, 75–77
Louisville, Ky., 34–35

Madison, James, 19
Maher, Bill, 128
Manchin, Joe, 128
Manson, Charles, 48, 50
Mao Zedong, 48
Mars Society, 123
Marx, Karl, 57, 114
Marxism, 3, 15–16, 36, 57–58,
	74, 76–78, 116, 120
"May 19 Communist
	Organization," 59
Mayorkas, Alejandro, 29, 32,
	77
McCarthy, Kevin, 40, 90
McConnell, Mitch, 18
Media, 34, 43, 58, 60, 62, 78, 91,
	99, 103, 104, 130, 135

Mein Kampf (Hitler), 86
Mexico and Mexicans, 29–31,
    53 (*See also* Southern
    border)
Miller, Christopher C., 42
Milley, Mark, 41–42
Minneapolis, Minn., 79–80
Minnesota, 33, 92, 93
Mississippi, 66
Moby Dick (Melville), 49
Money, as social glue, 114–115
Morality, 6, 100
MSNBC, 62, 111
Murder rate, 35
Music industry, 125–126
Musk, Elon, 122–125
Muslim Advocacy Day, 86
Muslim Brotherhood, 79, 82,
    85–86, 88–89
Muslim Students Association,
    84
Muslims, 20, 64, 79–89, 92 (*See
    also* Islamic terrorism)
Mystal, Elie, 111

NAACP, 98
The Nation, 111
National Guard, 42
National War Council, 51–54
Nazi Germany, 69, 85–86, 100,
    109, 115
NBC, 62
New Left, 10
New York City, 53, 54, 65–66
New York Post, 104
New York Times, 15, 54, 56,
    59–60, 62–63, 77, 90–91
NeXT, 122
Nicaragua, 136
9/11 terrorist attacks, 35, 82, 83,
    87, 89
"No Glory for Hate Act," 39
North Vietnam, 7

Nur, Mohamed, 78
Nyack, New York, 59

Obama, Barack, 5, 9–12, 29, 52,
    58, 81
Ocasio-Cortez, Alexandria, 78,
    85, 86, 91, 100
Oluo, Ijeoma, 76–77
Omar, Ilhan, 78–93, 117
O'Neal, Shaquille, 66
Orwell, George, 45
Orwellian Doublespeak, 61, 67

Palestinian Authority, 88, 92
Palestinians, 79, 84–86, 88, 90,
    92
Parks, Rosa, 98
PayPal, 123
Pelosi, Nancy, 39, 40, 44, 82, 84,
    87, 89–91, 136
Pentagon (*see* Department of
    Defense)
"People of color," 34, 58, 61–62,
    64–65, 77, 128–129
PepsiCo, 121
Pixar, 122
Planned Parenthood, 26–27
Plekhanov, Georgi, 7
Pompeo, Mike, 82
Poverty, 64, 67, 93, 112–113,
    132–135
Pressley, Ayanna, 78
Primitive Rebels (Hobsbawm),
    116
Profit motive, 125
Progressive Caucus, 117, 118
Progressives and progressivism,
    3–4, 9, 12–14, 16–18, 20,
    25–29, 32, 34, 37, 59, 62,
    65, 67–69, 73, 86–93, 99,
    110, 112, 114–119, 121,
    124–129, 131–136, 139
Pro-life movement, 26

Property ownership, 6
The Protocols of the Elders of
    Zion, 16
Pulitzer Foundation, 15
"Putin's price hike," 114

Quinnipiac University, 33
Qur'an, 88

Race Traitor (magazine), 54
Racists and racism:
    anti-Semitism, 84, 89–92,
        117, 120
    anti-white, 47–50, 53–69,
        74–75, 78, 80–82, 87, 92,
        111, 117, 118, 120, 131,
        132, 135–136
    of Black Lives Matter, 33–34
    demonization of right as,
        5–7, 12–21, 38, 99–102
    ideological, 91–93
    "systemic," 20, 34, 36, 56, 60,
        66
    white racism, 64, 66
Radicals and radicalism, 4–12,
    17, 20, 26, 47–48, 54,
    57–63, 69, 78, 81, 87,
    109–112, 120, 121, 130,
    140
Raskin, Jamie, 41
Re-education classes, 61
Religion, 139–140
Reparations for slavery, 13, 19,
    63, 116, 128
Republicans (Republican Party),
    11, 13–14, 16, 18, 39–41,
    60–61, 65, 84, 90, 97, 98,
    116, 136 (See also Trump,
    Donald)
Revolutions, 110
Robbins, Terry, 53, 54
Roe v. Wade, 26, 35–36
Rudd, Mark, 48–54, 59

Russia and Russians, 7, 37, 38,
    49, 98, 101, 102, 104, 114,
    116, 123–124, 136 (See
    also Soviet Union)

San Diego, Calif., 31
San Francisco, Calif., 59
Sánchez, Linda, 39
Sanders, Bernie, 30, 87, 89,
    118–122, 126–127
Sanger, Margaret, 23
Santa Fe, N.M., 53–54, 59
Sarsour, Linda, 91
Saudi Arabia, 83–84, 89
School voucher programs,
    134–135
Schumer, Chuck, 38
Sculley, John, 121–122
SDS (see Students for a
    Democratic Society)
Senate, 17, 38, 77
Senate Budget Committee, 118
Sicknick, Brian, 42–43
The 1619 Project, 15–16, 36, 74
60 Minutes, 33
Slavery and slave trade, 15–16,
    18–21, 63–64, 74, 130,
    132–133
Snoop Dogg, 67
So You Want to Talk About Race
    (Oluo), 76–77
"Social justice," 3, 4, 10, 12–14,
    16, 25, 56, 62, 63, 111–113,
    115–116, 126, 127
Socialism, 5, 9, 13, 14, 69, 109,
    110, 116–120, 122, 126, 136
Sociopathy, 27
Somalia, 78–80
Soros, George, 59
Southern border, 28, 29, 64, 129
Soviet Union, 78, 110, 120–121
    (See also Russia and
    Russians)

Space Force, 75–76
SpaceX, 123, 124
Spotify, 125–126
"The Squad," 30, 78, 84–86
Stalin, Joseph, 42, 116, 121
State Department, 73
"Stop and Frisk" laws, 63, 65–66
"Stop the Steal" speech (Trump),
    41
Student loans, 117–118
Student Nonviolent
    Coordinating Committee,
    120
Students for a Democratic
    Society (SDS), 47–48, 52,
    54
Students for Justice in Palestine,
    84
Supreme Court, 18, 26, 35–37,
    56, 131
"Systemic racism," 20, 34, 36, 56,
    60, 66

Taliban, 73–74, 77, 101
Tate, Sharon, 48, 50
Taylor, Breonna, 34–35
Teachers' unions, 135, 136, 139
Terrorists and terrorism:
    domestic, 20, 25, 76–78
    Islamic, 64, 73, 74, 79–90, 117
    the left as supporter of, 47,
        52, 59–60, 84–90, 92, 117
    Trump's attacks on, 99
    (See also 9/11 terrorist
    attacks)
Tesla, Inc., 123–124
Their Morals and Ours
    (Trotsky), 6
"Theory of intersectionality,"
    129–130
Thompson, Bennie, 43
Tlaib, Rashida, 78, 84–87, 90,
    117

Troi, Nguyen van, 7
Trotsky, Leon, 6
Trump, Donald, 14, 20, 28–30,
    37–43, 80, 81, 87–88, 95,
    97–105, 134–136
Trump Derangement Syndrome,
    95
Trump University, 101–102, 105
Twitter, 119

Ukraine, 101, 124
"Underserved communities," 61,
    68, 131
United Nations Development
    Plan, 78–79
United Packinghouse Workers,
    121
United States Treasury, 115
University of Chicago, 120
University of Pennsylvania,
    122–123
U.S. Coalition of Muslim
    Organizations, 86, 87
USSR (see Soviet Union)

Venezuela, 136
Vermont, 121
Vietnam War, 7–9, 50–51, 54, 59
Voter fraud, 36
Voter ID laws, 36

"War on Poverty," 112–113
Warren, Elizabeth, 26, 27, 30,
    88–89
Washington, George, 19
Washington Post, 63
Washington Times, 39
Wealth redistribution, 13, 14,
    57, 112–113, 115, 116, 119
Weathermen (Weather
    Underground), 47–49,
    51–55, 59, 69
Weimar Republic, 115

Weingarten, Benjamin, 91, 93
Welfare programs, 67, 112,
    133–134
West, Cornel, 54
West Bank, 86, 117
White Fragility (DiAngelo), 92
White racism, 64, 66
White skin privilege, 54–55, 60,
    62–67, 69
White supremacists (white
    supremacy), 12–15, 20,
    21, 36–38, 56, 60, 62, 69,
    74–78, 92, 98, 103, 115,
    128–129, 136
"Whiteness Studies," 58
Whites:
    anti-white racism, 47–50,
        53–69, 74–75, 78, 80–82,
        87, 92, 111, 118, 120, 131,
        132, 135–136

income levels of, 134–135
    as opponents of slavery and
        racism, 19, 20, 132–133
    as radicals, 47, 48
Wilson, Woodrow, 14
Winfrey, Oprah, 66
"Woke" progressives, 26
Women, 131–132
Women's March, 91
World War II, 117

X, Malcolm, 48
X.com, 123
Xendi, Ibram X., 93

Young Peoples Socialist League,
    120

Zionism, 120
Zip2, 123

ABOUT
THE AUTHOR

David Horowitz was born in 1939 to Communist parents. He was sent to The Sunnyside Progressive School when he was 18 months old and a Communist Party summer camp when he was six. He graduated Columbia University in 1959 and became an intellectual leader of the New Left with the publication of his first two books *Student* (1962) and *The Free World Colossus* (1965); the latter, an anti-American view of the Cold War.

In 1967, he became a senior editor of *Ramparts*, the largest magazine of the New Left. In 1971, with his friend Peter Collier and the support of a disgruntled staff, took control of *Ramparts* and ran it until 1973, when he and Collier left the magazine to write a *New York Times* bestseller on the Rockefellers, which was followed by a #1 *Times* bestseller on the Kennedys, and then another *Times* bestseller on the Fords.

By this time, Collier and Horowitz had undergone a sea of change politically, and not only departed the Left but regarded themselves as its nemeses. In a front page article in the *Washington Post*, they announced and justified the fact that both of them had voted for Ronald Reagan in the 1980 presidential election. In a separate book titled *Destruction*

Generation, they told their former comrades on the Left exactly what they thought of their sinister mission.

Horowitz is the founder of the David Horowitz Freedom Center and the *New York Times* bestselling author of many books, which have collectively sold more than a million copies. These include a two-volume autobiography—*Radical Son* and *Mortality and Faith*—a nine-volume series, *The Black Book of the American Left* and *The Enemy Within: How a Totalitarian Movement Is Destroying America*. He has also written such bestselling titles as *Big Agenda: President Trump's Plan to Save America, Blitz: Trump Will Smash the Left and Win, Dark Agenda: The War to Destroy Christian America*, and *Final Battle: The Next Election Could Be the Last*.